Sacred Tears

Sacred Tears

SENTIMENTALITY IN VICTORIAN
LITERATURE

FRED KAPLAN

PRINCETON, NEW JERSEY

PRINCETON UNIVERSITY PRESS

1987

Copyright © 1987 by Princeton University Press
Published by Princeton University Press,
41 William Street, Princeton, New Jersey 08540
In the United Kingdom: Princeton University Press,
Guildford, Surrey

All Rights Reserved

Library of Congress Cataloging in Publication Data will be found
on the last printed page of this book

ISBN 0-691-06700-7

This book has been composed in Linotron Bulmer

Clothbound editions of Princeton University Press
books are printed on acid-free paper, and binding
materials are chosen for strength and durability

Printed in the United States of America
by Princeton University Press
Princeton, New Jersey

To
Carl Woodring

Contents

Acknowledgments

Two extraordinary research institutions, the Huntington Library and the National Humanities Center, have supported me in my work on this and other books.

During 1981-1982, I had the advantage of the Huntington's archival resources, excellent librarians, and lovely sunshine. I am indebted to the former Director of the Library, James Thorpe, and to the Director of Research, Martin Ridge. I am also indebted to the Senior Research Fellows for inviting me to the Huntington, and to the staff for facilitating my work, particularly Librarian Daniel H. Woodward, Curator of Manuscripts Mary Robertson, Assistant Curator of Manuscripts Susan Hodson, Curator of Rare Books Alan Jutzi, Head of Reader Services Virginia I. Renner, Head of Photographic Services Robert Schlosser, and Assistant Curator of Art Shelley M. Bennett, as well as Harriet McLoone, Janet Hawkins, Susan Naulty, Barbara Quinn, Leona Schonfeld, Elsa Sink, and Doris Smedes. A version of Chapter 1 was presented as a Huntington lecture to the following colleagues, who, on this and other projects, were generous with both their suggestions and time: Leland Carlson, Horton Davies, John G. Demaray, Martha Demaray, Daniel Donno, Elizabeth Donno, Robert Halsband, Terry Kelly, Arthur Kinney, James Riddell, William A. Ringler, Jr., Hallett Smith, John M. Steadman, and Stanley Stewart.

An earlier version of Chapter 2 was given as a lecture at a meeting of the California Dickens Project at the University of California, Riverside, in 1983. I owe special thanks to my University of California colleagues on that project, particularly Murray Baumgarten, Edwin Eigner, and John Jordan, who have warmly supported and perceptively helped me in my work and in creating a national community of Dickens scholars.

Norman Fruman kindly read and commented on an earlier version of this book, and Jay Williams made many valuable suggestions.

I am particularly indebted to Mrs. Arthur Sherwood, now retired from her position as Literary Editor at Princeton University Press, for her interest in and support of this book, and for her many years of successful service to the Press and to the world of literary scholarship. Her successor, Robert E. Brown, has kindly and carefully seen this book through the Press. Janet Stern's expert copyediting has made the book more consistent and readable. Rhoda Weyr has helped in important ways. I thank Amy Robbins and Georges Borchardt, of Georges Borchardt, Inc., for their usual consideration and professionalism.

The creation and final revision of these Acknowledgments was done at the National Humanities Center, Research Triangle Park, North Carolina, where the Director, Charles Blitzer, and the Associate Director, Kent Mullikin, have created a research institution that does everything possible to encourage scholarship and writing. I owe them, and their associates, my deepest respect and appreciation.

Gloria Kaplan gave of her time and encouragement with perceptiveness, knowledgeability, and generosity.

It is to Carl Woodring that this book is dedicated, in appreciation for his decades of selfless service to our profession. My own debt is great; we shall not see his like again.

National Humanities Center
1986

Abbreviations

To minimize the number of endnotes in this book, I have used in the text abbreviations for the most frequently quoted works, followed by a reference to the chapter and/or page of the edition of the work (see Notes, p. 145) in which the particular citation is found. Following is a list of the abbreviations I have used.

DICKENS
DS   *Dombey and Son*
OMF   *Our Mutual Friend*

THACKERAY
EH   *The English Humourists of the Eighteenth Century*
VF   *Vanity Fair*
Pen   *Pendennis*
New   *The Newcomes*
HE   *Henry Esmond*

CARLYLE
CME   *Critical and Miscellaneous Essays*
HHW   *Heroes and Hero-Worship*
PP   *Past and Present*

Sacred Tears

Introduction

The subject of this book is of historical and contemporary importance. The canard that ours is an unsentimental and even anti-sentimental culture has been advanced by influential twentieth-century opinion makers. In modern high culture, sentimentality is often thought of as vaguely embarrassing or is condemned for being in bad taste or for being insincere. It can, of course, be all these things, but it need not necessarily be any of them. The success of the Royal Shakespeare Company's "sentimental" *Nicholas Nickleby* may have surprised some and distressed others, though those who were delighted far outnumbered those who were not. Neither Dickens nor his contemporaries would have been in the least surprised. Dickens believed that there was an instinctive, irrepressible need for human beings to affirm both in private and in public that they possessed moral sentiments, that these sentiments were innate, that they best expressed themselves through spontaneous feelings, and that sentimentality in life and in art had a moral basis. People—all people, except those who had been the victims of perverse conditioning or some misfortune of nature—instinctively felt, in Dickens' view, pleasure, *moral* pleasure, when those they thought of as good triumphed and those they thought of as bad were defeated. Most Victorians believed that the human community was one of shared moral feelings, and that sentimentality was a desirable way of feeling and of expressing ourselves morally.

This is a definition of human nature that not all of Dickens' contemporaries, let alone ours, agreed with. Its origin in our culture is eighteenth-century moral philosophy, with its optimistic view of human nature and human potential. The optimism of eighteenth-century moral philosophy was streaked

3

with dark shadows, both in life and in literature. Puritan and Hobbesian pessimism provided a constant counter-current. In the nineteenth century, and particularly among the Victorians, utilitarianism, rationalism, scientific determinism, and a weakening but still powerful Calvinism argued strongly against the moral sentiments. Still, much of popular culture then as now assumed that we do have innate moral sentiments, and that sentimentality is an expression of the basic nature of human nature. Most of the significant relationships and transactions of life appear, to many people, to be a response to instinctive moral feeling. Certainly the motivating force of the modern democratic ethos has been moral feeling, the felt conviction that we are to a considerable extent responsible for individual and communal welfare. Our society still functions, ultimately, on the belief that we know right from wrong through our innate feelings, and that, as Nicodemus Boffin says in Dickens' *Our Mutual Friend*, "It's a very good thing to think well of another person, and it's a very good thing to be thought well of by another person." He does not need to explain why.

This short study, the intent of which is to stimulate thought and suggest lines of further consideration, attempts to explain what it is Mr. Boffin thinks needs no explaining. Victorian culture, once the living inheritance of our parents and grandparents, has now become so distant that we cannot take for granted that we know the underlying assumptions made by Victorians about human nature and moral values. Without careful investigation and thought, we cannot know that we are even recognizing the assumptions that informed and gave communal significance to the bare statements that Victorian literature presents. Sometimes, indeed, we do not know that the Victorians meant this or that rather than something else, partly because we are misled by a common vocabulary into assuming that the words meant then what they do now, partly because post–World War II American and, to a lesser extent, British emphasis on critical reading and literary theory rather than on historical studies has produced many readings of Victorian literature that do not take into account crucial distinctions between Victorian and modern culture. Sometimes such conflations have been stimulating, even illuminating, especially about those aspects of Victorian literature that anticipate modern preoccupations, such as the prevalence of wasteland imagery, the emphasis on the alienated self, and the fascination with psychological states. The modernizing of Victorian literature, however, has had only limited success, leaving unilluminated numbers of key Victorian themes and patterns embedded so deeply in peculiarly Victorian values that modern preemption has proved impossible. One of these themes is Victorian sentimentality, a subject that many talk of though few speak well or sensibly about. There is little of value in print on the subject, and the purpose of this essay is to encourage a more informed and tolerant understanding and to stimulate more discussion of Victorian sentimentality by providing a brief introduction and a speculative theory that places Victorian sentimentality in the context of the history of ideas.

British Victorian sentimentality originated in eighteenth-century moral philosophy, particularly in the definitions of human nature offered by the major philosophers associated with the doctrine of the moral sentiments (or the moral affections) and benevolence. Consequently, Victorian sentimentality should not be evaluated in the terms offered by the mimetic tradition in both literature and the general culture, to which it is in fundamental, purposeful opposition, but as a protest against the increasingly powerful forces of philosophical and scientific realism that the intellectual community advanced but popular opinion rejected.

"Realism" is a hopelessly complicated term and subject. In literature, particularly in the novel, it stands for the use of devices of style and structure that stress the illusion that the world depicted by the author is governed by the same laws of cause and effect and the same conditions of physical concreteness that readers experience in their own lives. Philosophical realism is a broader phrase referring to various movements in interpreting life and reality that have as their basic principle that the world must be seen in practical, experiential terms, as it is, with all its mundane limitations, rather than through ideal, harmonizing constructs of the imagination, as we would like it to be. In the reductive terms of traditional textbook philosophy, the new Aristotelians opposed the new Platonists, philosophical realism denied the truth of traditional philosophical idealism. As a child of philosophical idealism, Victorian sentimentality defended the vision of the ideal against the claim that the universe and human history are governed by mechanical, or rational, or deterministic, or pragmatic forces; that we cannot maintain metaphysical or religious ideals; that all human nature is flawed; and that literature should not falsify life by depicting ideal characters and happy endings. Understood in the context of eighteenth-century moral philosophy, whose prime purpose was to adapt philosophical idealism to modern conditions, Victorian sentimentality, I suggest, was a late and occasionally shrill stage in a vigorous rear-guard action to defend human nature from further devaluation.

Chapter 1 presents the eighteenth-century background, the various philosophical and literary channels through which eighteenth-century ideas about human nature, especially in regard to the moral sentiments and sentimentality, became the assumptions, the working values, of many Victorian writers, particularly the two supreme novelists of the mid-century, Dickens and Thackeray. Lord Shaftesbury, Francis Hutcheson, Adam Smith, and David Hume provided the intellectual substructure for the widespread, popularly cherished Victorian belief that human beings are innately good, that the source of evil is malignant social conditioning, and that the spontaneous, uninhibited expression of the natural feelings (good because they are natural, good because we are by nature good) is admirable and the basis for successful human relationships. Such philosophical writings sometimes influenced the Victorians directly. Dickens, Thackeray more so, and Carlyle extensively, read the moral philosophers. Still, much of the tone and substance of this optimistic view of human nature and the role of the sentiments flowed into the Victorian consciousness indirectly through the influential, widely read masters of eighteenth-century literature, especially Pope, Fielding, Richardson, and Goldsmith, who are the literary side of the coin of moral philosophy, and who had immense impact on the Victorians.

Chapter 2 focuses on Dickens. The most widely read Victorian writer in our time, he is so prominently associated with both the blessings and the banes of sentimentality that it seems sensible to highlight his practices and views on the subject. Dickens' sentimentality is a joy to those who respond to it but an embarrassment to those whose sense of taste and reality it offends. For those conditioned by the rigors of modernism and any of the varieties of philosophical realism, the master has been flawed by the moral and aesthetic vice of sentimentality. Dickens' genius, though, is deeply embedded in his belief in the moral sentiments and cannot, I believe, be comprehended outside of its Victorian idealistic assumptions, complicated and inconsistent as they are. As we try to understand Dickens' sentimentality, it is important that we understand his indebtedness to Goldsmith and Wordsworth, the moral significance of his treatment of death, his awareness of the potential gap between feelings and moral acts, his corresponding concern with "benevolence" as a means of closing that gap, and the irresolvable problems he confronted in his efforts to provide moral paradigms in his fiction to compensate for their absence in society.

Chapters 3 and 4 deal with Thackeray, emphasizing in particular *Vanity Fair* and *The English Humourists of the Eighteenth Century*. Modern readings of Thackeray tend to transform him, at worst into a cynic about human nature, at best into an embodiment of modern ambivalence. But, despite his "irony," his "realism," and his alleged "cynicism," Thackeray was as much a sentimentalist in his view of human nature and its moral instincts as was Dickens. In contrast, Carlyle, the subject of Chapter 5, became the spokesman for those ambivalent Victorians who anticipated the twentieth-century renunciation of sentimentality without being immune to, let alone liberated from, the feelings to which sentimentality appeals. Carlyle was hostile to sentimentality mainly because he associated it with sensuality, particularly in fiction, and with a definition of human nature that is secular and ethical rather than transcendental and spiritual, though his emphasis on his own feelings as self-evidently moral and his dependence on moral ideals in his depiction of the hero have sentimental dimensions. Carlyle attempted to reject sentimentality without also rejecting philosophical idealism, partly because, unlike so many Victorians, he believed that sentimentality corrupted rather than supported philosophical idealism, partly because he could not accept the beneficent view of human nature that moral philosophy presented. He sensed that Dickens and Thackeray, given the assumptions of sentimentality, strained to account—or failed to account satisfactorily—for the existence of evil.

Except for Wordsworth, whose own roots were firmly embedded in eighteenth-century moral philosophy, the major Romantic writers played no significant role in the formation of the Victorian attitude toward sentimentality. The Romantics have been loosely described as exponents of a religion of the heart and of a psychology of the sensibility. Except for Wordsworth, I doubt that the former is true, and that the latter is correct corroborates my claim that the Romantics in general are neither the source of nor correlatives for Victorian sentimentality. Romantic sensibility is not congenial either to eighteenth-century moral philosophy or to Victorian sentimentality. The Romantic idealization of sensibility came through Rousseau, Sterne, and Mackenzie. The tear-filled worship of sacred sentimentality in Victorian culture came through the philosophy and literature of the moral sentiments that the early Victorians read, studied, and breathed as their childhood air. Since Wordsworth is the Romantic poet whose feelings and ideas the Victorians most deeply inhaled, it is not surprising that the Wordsworthian elements in the Victorian sentimental writers support and confirm the definition of human nature and the doctrine of the moral sentiments that the Victorians derived from their eighteenth-century idols. For the purpose of understanding Victorian sentimentality, it is as if the Romantics, with the exception of Wordsworth, hardly existed. Life and influence came from the grandfathers rather than from the fathers.

Since this is a speculative essay, I hope that the broad overview I present in Chapter 1 and the emphasis on Dickens, Thackeray, and Carlyle throughout will encourage others to expand the survey to include Brontë, Trollope, George Eliot, and Victorian popular literature. Dickens, Thackeray, and Carlyle do, I believe, represent the various levels and the dominant patterns of Victorian literary culture as a whole. Two of them were the most popular serious novelists of the early and mid-Victorian years; Carlyle was the most influential writer of nonfictional prose, and his impact can be located in the special genius of his works rather than in a broadly based popular tradition. Each in his distinctive way expresses the Victorian attempt to come to terms with the definition of human nature and the values of sentimentality derived from eighteenth-century moral philosophy. Each expresses both the pains and the pleasures of the challenge. I do, of course, make brief comments on numbers of other Victorian writers. But my interest is more in theory than in praxis, and it may be that the author who one day undertakes the definitive survey of the subject will find this speculative essay a helpful point of departure.

The Moral Sentiments

◆━━◆◎◆ 1 ◆◎◆━━◆

All human nature is mixed, Henry Fielding wrote in *Tom Jones* (1749), a favorite novel of both Dickens and Thackeray. "Life most exactly resembles the stage, since it is often the same person who represents the villain and the hero; and he who engages your admiration today will probably attract your contempt tomorrow. . . . A single bad act no more constitutes a villain in life than a single bad part on the stage."[1] Apparently Fielding believed that "human nature" is an entity that, in the tradition of faculty psychology, can be reified from observable qualities and actions. Modern readers are not likely to be as certain as Fielding about what this "human nature" is or even *if* it is. Even the esteemed *Encyclopedia of Philosophy* has not attempted to define the protean phrase, while the *Oxford English Dictionary* is remarkably weak in its historical presentation of the multitudinous uses of the phrase. That all human beings, with the rarest of exceptions, contain both attractive and unattractive, constructive and destructive elements has become a truism of modern culture, whose tolerance for idealizations and personifications in life and in art has been declining noticeably since the eighteenth century. When dealing with "human nature" as a phenomenon and as an explanation of behavior, modern democratic society as a whole desires to be as inclusive as possible while at the same time protecting itself from both criminals and saints.

Fielding himself raised the standard of normative probability in regard to everything, and especially in regard to "human nature." Even his idealized characters, like Sophia Western and Squire Allworthy in *Tom Jones*, are partly shaped under the pressure of literary realism. The increasingly strong tradition of literary and philosophical realism from the eighteenth century on raised questions of human definition that came to be widely addressed; philosophy, through much of the eighteenth and a good part of the nineteenth century, was moral philosophy and psychology. By the late nineteenth century, though, even those most idealistic about human nature and least satisfied with behavioral definitions were likely to agree with Fielding's inference that you cannot build castles in the mud without getting your hands dirty. Robert Browning dramatically condemns his "Pictor Ignotus" (Unknown Painter) of 1845 who has declined to use his immense artistic talents because he fears and condemns the mixed nature of human beings.

> Blown harshly, keeps the trump its golden cry?
> Tastes sweet the water with such specks of earth?
> (ll. 71-72)

⌘———❦ 2 ❧———⌘

Most of the writers and philosophers of what is sometimes prejudicially called the Enlightenment took a positive, rather optimistic view of "human nature." They had no doubt that such an entity existed, and that it could be described in normative terms that applied to the generality of mankind, as the innate disposition or character of individuals and of humankind as a whole. Tradition and the force of belief compelled them to assume that mankind had a maker, though considerable difference of opinion existed about the form and the qualities of the maker, and about the relationship between the maker and the made. But it was widely believed that the maker's greatest creation, humankind, a subdivision of Nature or the total creation, had been endowed with certain inalienable qualities shared by the entire species which could, sensibly and logically, be called "human nature," to differentiate it, for example, from animal nature. At this high level of discussion, then, one could talk about human nature without referring to particular examples, which might or might not prove the rule. For the rule, whose broad features controlled all discussions and depictions of human beings, existed prior to examples, all of which stretched back in a long line to Adam and Eve, to Biblical character typology. The popular imagination then, as now, had no doubt that human character was stable, archetypal, and universal. In the Enlightenment, the educated elite, despite considerable variety of opinion in many areas, generally accepted that "human nature" was an identifiable entity, a real thing, and that it could be defined in universally applicable abstract terms.

Eighteenth-century moral optimism created an exaggerated sunshine in which human nature glowed, and whose brightness much of modern culture has found unacceptably monochromatic. Some of that sunshine glowed from the emerging secular idealism and gradual tilt through the age of revolution toward democracy and a redefinition of human nature that for the first time included human rights. Of course, eighteenth-century British culture had its somber, even dark, views and visions as well. In *Gulliver's Travels* (1726), Swift makes dramatically persuasive the king of Brobdingnagia's condemnatory definition of humankind as "the most pernicious race of odious vermin that Nature ever suffered to crawl on the face of the earth." Samuel Johnson viewed human nature as innately flawed—even sanity itself was constantly threatened by a natural predisposition to excess and madness—and to speak only of eighteenth-century optimistic views of human nature would be to distort the complex reality by stressing only the dominant tendency.

Strong forces in the Enlightenment—of religion, of philosophy, even of popular culture—resisted moral idealism. The arguments of the most influential moral philosophers, such as Lord Shaftesbury, Henry St. John, Francis Hutcheson, David Hume, and Adam Smith, are informed and invigorated by their awareness of the somber opposition, Calvinistic, theocratic, aristocratic, evangelical, mathematical, and even economic. Whether directly acknowledged or not, the influential phrases of Thomas Hobbes in *Leviathan* (1651) cast a formidable shadow over the next two centuries.

> For the laws of nature—as *justice, equity, modesty, mercy*, and, in sum, *doing to others as we would be done to*—of themselves, without the terror of some power to cause them to be observed, are contrary to our natural passions, that carry us to partiality, pride, revenge, and the like. And covenants without the sword are but words, and of no strength to secure a man at all.[2]

Hobbes's overpowering darkness could be lightened only by an exaggerated brightness, a spotlight so bright that it could illumine his darkness. Eighteenth-century optimism is to a considerable extent a reaction against the Hobbesian view of a viciously flawed human nature, which only a repressive state can control and only a god of grace can redeem. Such a dim view of human nature represents the secularization of the Puritan vision, which was based, after all, on daily experience as well as on universal rules about fallen human nature in a fallen world. The Puritan view seemed at times an effective, experiential definition of human nature based on observation of the "pernicious race."

It is precisely this view that the Enlightenment as a cultural movement attempted to reject. Of course, both Puritan and Enlightenment culture tended to evaluate human action in moral terms. Fielding and his latitudinarian contemporaries were as compulsive on such matters as the Puritans, though the tone is noticeably different. Fielding and his contemporaries expressed a very unpuritanical genial tolerance for "natural Imperfections," mainly because they believed in a cosmic framework that absorbed moral flaws into a benign social structure.[3] Nevertheless, on the middle ground of moral performance, the Puritan and Enlightenment cultures were in fundamental agreement on the necessity for a personal and communal code of behavior whose ultimate authentication is the Judaeo-Christian prescription of love, justice, and harmony.

The pervasive challenge for Enlightenment as well as Puritan culture was to interpret and explain immoral rather than moral performance, partly because of its prevalence, partly because it fascinates in a way that moral performance does not. The construct "human nature" needed to be further explored, its mysteries made clear, its basic elements revealed. On the success of this venture depended the earthly paradise or the heavenly city or both, if one's philosophy could contain both. Fielding attempted to explain corrupt actions as consistent with the "natural Imperfections" of human nature, part of his socially oriented theological view of the cosmos in which the emphasis is on the Enlightenment's earthly paradise. His Puritan predecessors and contemporaries, with an emphasis on the heavenly city, explained the same acts as the result of the fallen condition of human nature. Whatever the definition and explanation of human nature, the need to explain and the hope that a satisfactory explanation could be constructed dominated much that was thought and written in British culture at least until the middle of the nineteenth century. The declining interest in modern culture, outside of religious communities, in explaining either moral or immoral performance probably results from the loss of any credible standard against which to evaluate it, and from a reversion to the folk wisdom that holds that such evaluations tend to be reductive. In general, the modern response to nastiness is either active opposition or a stoical reference to "human nature."

⌎——⧫ 3 ⧫——⌏

Sentimentality in the Western tradition takes its force from a keen awareness of the mixed nature of human nature. It is an attempt, among other things, to generate or at least to strengthen the possibility of the triumph of the feelings and the heart over self-serving calculation. As an offspring of Enlightenment optimism, sentimentality assumes the existence of innate "moral sentiments." Historically, sentimentality found its propitious moment when both the latitudinarian and Puritan explanations of human nature were losing their effectiveness and the possibility of comprehensive alternative explanations, particularly of good and evil, seemed dim. Sentimentality promised to locate the grounds of moral performance in feelings, innate moral feelings, without demanding that these moral feelings produce moral actions (though the desirability of such a result was central to the Victorian con-

16

sciousness), and without demanding that a belief in the centrality of moral feeling necessitated a comprehensive theory of human nature or of the cosmos that explained all mysteries and resolved all inconsistencies.

Many people, some of them rather admirable, both in the past and in the present have used the word as if being sentimental were a virtue, though often with no sense of an obligation to define its meaning or explain the significance of the concept. The *Oxford English Dictionary* presents a reasonably clear history of the term. The word *sentiment* came into English as early as the fourteenth century and meant (in chronological sequence) "one's own feelings," "physical feeling," "mental attitude (of approval or disapproval)," "an emotion," "a thought or reflection coloured by or proceeding from emotion," "an emotional thought expressed in literature or art," and "a striking or agreeable thought or wish." The words *sentimental* and *sentimentality* were coined in the middle to late eighteenth century to indicate something "characterized by sentiment" and "the quality of being sentimental," respectively. Throughout the eighteenth century and through much of the nineteenth, neither word had pejorative implications, except in special cases. With slowly gathering force, *sentimentalism* came to denote late in the nineteenth century the misuse of sentiment, "the disposition to attribute undue importance to sentimental considerations, to be governed by sentiment in opposition to reason; the tendency to excessive indulgence in or insincere display of sentiment." The word sentiment and its various forms could still be used non-pejoratively, as in James Anthony Froude's remark that "a nation with whom sentiment is nothing is on its way to cease to be a nation at all." But the notion of sentimentality as insincerity, as false feeling, even as hypocrisy, became increasingly strong.

Though popular culture—and social and political life in general—kept its heart beating with the blood of sentimentality, intellectual modernism and modern high art stigmatized sentimentality as the refuge of philistinism and small minds. Sentimentality was not moral because it was not an expression of true feeling, of natural feeling, and the feelings themselves were not a reliable guide to moral action. The notion of unearned and undisciplined feeling, and the fear of a dangerous misperception of the role of feeling in life in general, reached back to infect with distasteful overtones and to distort ahistorically the eighteenth- and nineteenth-century definitions of sentiment and sentimentality.[4]

The eighteenth-century writers most responsible for imposing moral value on "sentiment" were David Hume and Adam Smith. In his *Essays and Treatises* (1758) and especially in his discussion of the passions in *Treatise of Human Nature* (1739–1740), Hume argued that "the ultimate ends of human actions can never . . . be accounted for by *reason*, but recommend themselves entirely to the sentiments and affections of mankind, without any dependence on the intellectual faculties," and that inherent within all human beings is "some internal taste or feeling . . . which distinguishes moral good and evil, and which embraces the one and rejects the other."[5] Hume stressed that we act not on the basis of thought but of feeling, and that we all possess a moral "sentiment" that we get pleasure from responding to. Hume's optimistic definition of human nature has its complement in Adam Smith's. In *The Theory of Moral Sentiments* (1759), Smith created the genial metaphor of the "internal . . . impartial spectator," the "man within the breast," a second self that we all possess, against whose altruistic and benevolent standards we judge our thoughts and actions. This better self serves as an internalized guide and self-corrector, a projection of our innate moral sentiments.[6]

The value of sentiment and its positive connotation in eighteenth-century definitions of human nature, such as Hume's and Smith's, have been obscured to many modern readers in a way that they were not to the Victorians. Part of the confusion results from confounding *sentiment* with *sensibility*, the latter connected with the eighteenth-century emphasis on "the man of feeling." The "man of feeling" developed into the Romantic hero of sensibility. The "man of sentiment" developed into the Victorian hero of the good and the moral heart. Some of the classic texts of eighteenth-century literature have contributed to modern obfuscation about the meaning of sentiment and sentimentality to eighteenth- and nineteenth-century readers. Lawrence Sterne's *A Sentimental Journey* (1759) tempts readers to assume that the feelings are discontinuous, disjointed, even anarchic, and that sexual passion is an expression of sensibility that need not recognize moral and social restraints. Henry Mackenzie's depiction in *The Man of Feeling* (1771) of a sensibility too refined for active engagement with a coarse society may be taken as a claim that sentiment is asocial or antisocial. And even Oliver Goldsmith's *The Vicar of Wakefield* (1776), an influential favorite of the Victorians and widely acknowledged to be a powerful teacher of virtue, may contribute to the modern confusion about eighteenth- and nineteenth-century definitions of sentiment since, in that novel, moral sentiment frequently seems to be misapplied to unworthy recipients or, even worse, to be the grounds for self-punishment.

Both Hume and Smith believed that an access of feeling cannot be an excess of feeling. Feeling cannot be self-destructive or socially harmful unless it is divorced from the other attributes of human nature inherent in all human beings. In that context, there can be no excess, or even misapplication, of feeling, for the basic nature of human nature is moral. The moral sentiments are a constituent, a given part of us, whether we will or no. The more responsive we are to our moral feelings, the better, the more moral, our individual and social conduct will be. The question of sensibility in the Romantic sense and of sentimentality in the modern sense of falsification of feeling has no meaning in this context. On the contrary, it is the absence of the expression of moral feeling and the restriction and denial of the value of sentimentality that are unnatural, that are falsifications of reality.

◦——◦◦ 4 ◦◦——◦

Some of the major Victorian writers read Hume and Smith, and some occasionally read Shaftesbury and Hutcheson. But whatever the philosophical and literary resources available to them—from the book-laden shelves of Thomas Arnold's library at Rugby to the few portable items in the suitcases of the Dickens family—the Victorian poets and novelists were shaped more by the popular literature they read and by the temper of the times than by any formal attempt to master the "thought" of the previous century. Thackeray vigorously attests to the pervasive influence of Swift, Fielding, Sterne, and Goldsmith, though he rather regrets that Hogarthian earthiness had been excised from the legacy. Dickens, like Thackeray, acknowledges how important his reading of eighteenth-century fiction was to the formation of his values and his definition of human nature. Carlyle, in response to his extensive reading of eighteenth-century literature, including Hume and the other moral philosophers, rebels against the values and the rhetoric of sentimentality in ways that reveal how inescapable its influence was. His reading in his formative years of eighteenth-century fiction, with its advocacy of the moral sentiments, probably contributed to his hostility to Victorian fiction which seemed to him to advocate no philosophy at all.

Carlyle's predilection for moral idealizations prompted him to contrast favorably the seriousness of Goethe's *Wilhelm Meister* with Victorian fictional entertainments. Art was the business of philosophers, of serious minds. Victorian fiction neglected the crucial issues of nature, human nature, and the moral foundation of the human situation. It lacked moral earnestness and intellectual seriousness. Its sentimentality expressed its moral and intellectual superficiality. That he himself also had absorbed into his basic values and his literary-philosophical ideas some of the assumptions and structures of moral philosophy and the moral sentiments did not prevent him from denouncing and dismissing the sentimentality of his contemporaries. And, like the great propagandists of literature, he exaggerated for pedagogic purposes, intent on playing the gadfly to secular humanism and liberal Protestantism. Dickens recognized and valued Carlyle's penchant for calculated distortion about genre and principles. As with his jeremiads against authority, democracy, and social disorder, such distortions were dangerous only if not properly discounted and irrelevant only if taken literally. Carlyle himself, like Dickens and Thackeray, had found his earliest instruction among the delights of Defoe, Smollett, and Fielding. And the "cloud-capped towers" of Shakespeare's art always remained for him more engaging than expository philosophy.

Eighteenth-century moral philosophy primarily made its way into the Victorian consciousness through the works of the great writers of eighteenth-century fiction, particularly Defoe, Fielding, Richardson, and Goldsmith. One poet, however, made a substantial contribution. Alexander Pope was the Victorian's "Philosopher, Guide, and Friend," the *vade mecum* of available insight, expressed in the pithy wisdom of closed couplets, on matters of human nature and the human situation. Dickens and many of his contemporaries were certain that it was not true in regard to social conditions that "Whatever is, is RIGHT." But they did aspire to share, without always being successful, Pope's conviction that some "Eternal Art" is "educing good from ill." Dickens found Pope's combination of social satire and universal optimism an attractive model. So too did Tennyson, who transformed universal optimism into visionary transcendence, screened by a degree of social indifference that Dickens never felt and could never afford. Pope's confidence that God has a firm grip on his universe seemed dubious to Carlyle, whose definition of life as conflict and history as revelation could never admit of certainty about local providence. But even Thackeray's low opinion of "Vanity Fair," where there are no heroes, did not prevent his extolling Pope's *Dunciad*, in which "heroic courage" speaks and "truth, the champion, shining and intrepid," fights "a wonderful and victorious single combat in that great battle which has always been waging since society began."[7] Dickens and Thackeray embraced Pope's claim that, despite man's mixed nature and state,

> Vice is a monster of so frightful mien,
> As, to be hated, needs but to be seen.[8]

In the area of human definition, Pope's phrase from the *Essay on Man*, "the surest virtues thus from passions shoot," provided the Victorian focus, as it provided the focus for Fielding's *Tom Jones* and Richardson's *Clarissa*.[9]

Of the eighteenth-century novelists widely read by the Victorians, only Defoe depicted the Hobbesian world of suspicion about human nature and dramatized its faulty moral potential. It was not a view that eighteenth-century moral philosophy and the schools of sentimentality which developed from it found attractive. Despite the widespread recognition among the Victorians of Defoe's merits as a craftsman and the power of his depiction of a world fallen from grace, his appeal was mainly to the nonconformist world, effectively displaced from the center of the stage of English letters by the dominance of Anglican mainstream culture. Radical Protestantism is more often than not the object of satire in Victorian literature, in Emily Brontë, Browning, Dickens, Eliot, Arnold, and Trollope, or disregarded, as if outside the pale of civilized consciousness, in Thackeray and Tennyson.

As has often been noted, Defoe's works give fictional embodiment to the Puritan ethos. Everything that happens to his characters is the "merciful Disposition of Providence," which determines and controls individual and social life in its minutest particulars.[10] Human nature, an actor in a universal drama, is sinful because the terms of the drama, the words of the given script, demand that it be so. The feelings of the actors in the drama are part of their fallen nature, their worst part, not their best. For Defoe, feeling and passion are indistinguishable, and it is the failure of right reason or sound judgment in the face of the strength of the passions that is the sign of the devil within us. In the world of *Moll Flanders*, our "Natures" are "capable of so much Degeneracy." Passion constantly overwhelms reason, for all human passions come from "the Devil in the inside of man."[11] In Defoe's depiction of "human nature," his characters can take neither blame nor credit for the ethical content of their thoughts and deeds.

Moll's consciousness has been made a battleground in a conflict in which she is an involuntary participant. External factors determine the result. But, since human consciousness is the battleground in this internalized conflict, Defoe's people find it difficult if not impossible to take a neutral attitude toward the participants. They must sign on with either Satan or God. The stakes, then, become as high for the battleground, for human beings, as for the prime antagonists, though Defoe's people are not themselves responsible for the existence of the conflict and the conditions under which it is fought. And, of course, they bear no responsibility for the final outcome, which has already been determined by supernatural powers.

Defoe, then, has little interest in "Human Nature" but a great deal of interest in human consciousness. Defoe's people do not have innate moral sentiments; all human feeling is contaminated by passion. Moll's feelings play no role in determining her destiny, and whether she acts morally, defined in theological terms, depends on the outcome of the battle between God and the Devil rather than on the qualities of her human nature. All human emotions are witnesses, not sources. Even repentance, the gift of grace, is not the triumph of innate moral feeling. It is a step in an externally controlled process in which feeling plays the role of witness, not author. In that sense, Moll is a plastic creature. Her "nature" is distinct from her personality, the former a predetermined vehicle in a cosmic competition, the latter a triumph of Defoe's artistry.

Whether moral feeling is a volitional element perplexed, sometimes even distressed, some Victorian writers who found themselves engaged in bitter conflict with the Puritan legacy represented by Defoe. The evangelical counterrevolution against latitudinarian views had great force in Britain during the first half of the nineteenth century. Many of the major Victorian writers found evangelical doctrine and rhetoric frighteningly authoritarian, and, though evangelicalism and Romanticism sometimes seemed curiously similar, the role of the heart in evangelical conversion was more like Defoe's witness to grace than like Romantic notions of the heart as the seat of moral feeling and the source of moral performance.

Despite Shaftesburyan optimism meeting keen resistance from social liberals on the one hand and evangelical revisionists on the other, even those Victorian writers who had reservations about the innate moral nature of human nature maintained the ideal as a model. Carlyle, for instance, the most Puritan of the important Victorian writers, whose authoritarian impulses made his liberal Protestant friends uneasy, believed that human feelings are the source of belief rather than that belief determines the value of human feelings. Though he responded to his Puritan heritage strongly enough to absorb some of its views and much of its tone, Carlyle nevertheless believed that some people at least do have innate moral sentiments. Certainly "heroes" do. And he did have a firm sense that there is an entity that can be called "human nature." It works in mysterious ways, an essential element in the complicated miracle of creation, and human beings have a degree of control over and hence responsibility for its performance. The strength of Carlyle's expressed detestation of eighteenth-century mechanism and secularism should not obscure the subtle ways in which Hume, Smith, and the moral philosophers in general qualify his Puritanism and influence his view of human nature.

Shaftesbury's optimism resulted from his belief that human well-being and happiness are within our potential because human beings are endowed by a benevolent creator with innate good impulses, which align our personal well-being with the well-being of the community. All "our happiness depends on natural and good affection." Still, the "affections," which are the source of our morality, must be guided by judgment to enable us to distinguish between the "self-passions," which are unnatural in that they are not conducive to our well-being, and our moral feelings.[12] In the view of the moral philosophers, human beings have been given an innate moral sense, which operates as feeling rather than as thought. "We conclude," Hutcheson wrote, "that all Men have the same Affections and Senses." The dangerous passions, which Hobbes fears, which Defoe believes are the expressions of the Devil, can readily be brought to heel by the natural affections acting in consonance with sound judgment.

> How can any one look upon this World as under the direction of an evil Nature or even question a perfectly good PROVIDENCE? How clearly does the Order of our Nature point out to us our true Happiness and Perfection, and lead us to it as naturally as the several Powers of the Earth, the Sun, and Air, bring Plants to their Growth, and the Perfection of their kinds? . . . Is not . . . our Nature admonished, exhorted and commanded to cultivate universal Goodness and Love, by a Voice heard thro' all the Earth, and Words sounding to the Ends of the World?[13]

Hume, who changed the word "affections" into "sentiment," strengthened the claim made by Shaftesbury and Hutcheson in the war against Hobbesian pessimism and Puritan determinism. What matters most is that human beings give their innate feelings the opportunity to determine their actions rather than permit actions to be determined by external forces, whether theological or secular. Like Shaftesbury, Hume desired to give perniciousness and the unruly passions sufficient recognition so that the doctrine of innate moral sentiments would not be undermined by the widespread sense gained from general experience that virtue does not have an easy time of it. But it is the innate "sentiments" that provide the decisive blow in the victory of goodness. Neither "reason" nor "utility" can provide it. For "in all moral decisions," it is "sentiment" that gives "preference to the useful above the pernicious tendencies. This sentiment can be no other," Hume claims, "than a feeling for the happiness of mankind, and a resentment of their misery, since these are the different ends which virtue and vice have a tendency to promote."[14]

The "sentiment" that Hume believes promotes "the happiness of mankind" Fielding locates in and makes identical with the "good heart." The "good heart" is not an organ but a given tendency to react with moral feeling. Neither education nor theology provides or accounts for it. All human beings have the potential for it, though its effective realization is sometimes balked by a pernicious environment or by other qualities. All human nature is mixed, Fielding exclaims, though he dramatizes, paradoxically, in *Joseph Andrews* and *Tom Jones*, a world in which some human natures are mixed and a few are absolutely good. Those that are mixed, driven by the half-yoke of realism, derive their unattractive characteristics from the misfortunes of their environment or the mysteries of genetic deprivation. But whatever has gone wrong proves an instructive complement to what has gone right: Black George is outbalanced by Partridge, Blifel by Tom. Ultimately, ill nature is in the service of good nature, and good nature, the visible representation of the moral sentiments, is an innate quality of "Mankind." Fielding indeed assumes that he has "good-natur'd Reader[s]" who by nature will feel pleasure in virtue and hostility to vice.[15]

Claims of the ideal in a mixed world are, of course, difficult to maintain, and Fielding creates irony and comedy in dramatizing the ideal, aware of the satiric potential in the interaction between characters whose natures are absolutely good and those whose natures are sufficiently mixed so that they cannot be relied on to act well always. In *Joseph Andrews*, Parson Adams gracelessly assaults a resisting world with his innate goodness, and the idealized Adams and the unidealized mixed nature of humankind effectively neutralize one another. The conflict is benign, the result is comedy, and in the end a model of harmony—a reconciliation of the ideal with the real—emerges. And even Parson Adams's goodness is a manifestation of sentiment, not philosophy, of innate feeling rather than doctrine. After preaching stoical resignation to Joseph, who believes that Fanny is being raped, Adams bursts into hysterical lamentation at the report, fortunately false, that his son has drowned.[16] Fielding is aware, of course, that the ideal has inherent difficulties for the novelist, who is under the constant pressure of verisimilitude, no matter how determined his efforts to manipulate or even defy the demands of realism. He feels the inescapability of the standard of the probable, the possible, and the marvelous. Parson Adams' innate goodness may be drafted into the army of the probable only if humanizing and comically acceptable "imperfections" accompany its service. And yet Fielding demonstrates how strongly committed he is to the ideal and how difficult of realization ideal characters are in literature in his creation of Sophia, who exists to demonstrate that the ideal must be the model for all human aspirations.

Why Fanny, Joseph, and Parson Adams in *Joseph Andrews*

and Tom, Sophia, Mrs. Nightingale, and the narrator in *Tom Jones* have good hearts and innate moral sentiments to a degree that distinguishes them from much of the rest of humankind Fielding does not elucidate other than to imply that he believes in a hierarchy of natural goodness. For example, Thwakum can thwack and Square can square until doomsday: they cannot destroy or even modify Tom's innate goodness. And Blifel can read sound doctrine and study moral philosophy endlessly without improving his moral nature. Fielding seems to believe that there are innate differences from birth in the degree of moral sentiment human beings possess, though, conveniently, characters in his novels usually rise in the social scale to the level that their innate qualities deserve. Once error and confusion have been resolved, inherited social position and moral qualities generally turn out to be consonant with one another. Fortunately, Fielding is incapable of absolute consistency on this point, and in minor characters, such as Partridge and Mrs. Nightingale, who possess good hearts, Fielding quietly reminds us and himself that the moral ideal and social position do not always dovetail. But he is still far from the ethos that compels Dickens to separate the moral sentiments from middle or high birth, and he is especially distant from the view of human nature that enables Dickens to depict Nancy in *Oliver Twist* and Martha in *David Copperfield* as versions of Sophia. Despite low birth and battered lives as prostitutes, they have innate moral sentiments and are admirable people.

Samuel Richardson's impact on Victorian literature, particularly on the novelists, was more powerful than even Fielding's, partly because he framed the central questions about human nature, the moral sentiments, and sentimentality in ways that were more directly accessible both to his contem-

poraries and to the Victorians. Fielding's novels are narrated
through a character once removed, the author-narrator. Richardson's novels are dramatic narratives, mostly in the words of
the participating characters. Despite his commitment to the
moral sentiments, Fielding made his appeal to the heart
through the head. Richardson made his appeal to the heart
through the heart, through a heightening of feeling in the
first-person drama of the epistolary novel. For this and other
reasons Richardson was a part of popular culture in a way that
Fielding was not, and he was closer to the popularization of
the doctrine of the moral sentiments that made the sentimental novel and "being sentimental" fashionable by the middle
of the eighteenth century. Richardson may have appreciated
the irony of one of his sympathetic readers asking him to define "sentimental," a word

> so much in vogue amongst the polite, both in town and
> country. . . . I have asked several who make use of it, and
> have generally received for answer, it is—it is—senti-
> mental. Everything clever and agreeable is compre-
> hended in that word; but am convinced a wrong inter-
> pretation is given, because it is impossible everything
> clever and agreeable can be so common as this word. I
> am astonished to hear such a one is a sentimental man;
> we were a sentimental party; I have been taking a sen-
> timental walk . . . I had just received a sentimental
> letter.[17]

That Richardson had published two years earlier a novel,
Clarissa, that elevated the ideal and depicted the tragic consequences of subordinating moral sentiment to "everything"
that society thinks "clever and agreeable" did not discourage
Lady Bradshaigh from addressing her question to him.

She was partly right in asserting Richardson's authority on the subject. Whether he intended it or not, he made it easy for his readers to separate the religious substance of Clarissa's feelings from the dramatic expression of the feelings themselves.

There is no evidence that Richardson read Shaftesbury and Hutcheson or that he had the slightest conceptual interest in moral philosophy. But neither was he by education or by values a Hobbesian. In fact, the forces in *Clarissa* that embody Hobbesian power and *Realpolitik*, particularly Clarissa's father, brother, and sister, are purposely presented as repugnant manifestations of the middle-level authoritarianism that Hobbes's view of human nature promotes. Richardson's Anglicanism is more somber than Fielding's, more inclined to envision human nature and dramatic conflict in Manichaean terms that are Miltonic and Puritanical. Clarissa and Lovelace are like God and Satan in conflict. Still, their allegorical rigor is constantly softened by their sentiments, particularly Clarissa's, and even Lovelace is a creature ultimately consumed by the power of his own feelings unrestrained by judgment. The other characters in the novel seem remarkably like those in Fielding's novels, embodiments of the mixed nature of human nature. They live in a normative world that affirms the possibility of the moral sentiments while recognizing the powerful limitations imposed on their expression by contingent circumstances.

Richardson helped establish the popular and loose expression of sentimentality that Lady Bradshaigh protested against by his convincing depiction of the feelings as the dominant mode of learning and being in *Clarissa*. But the implications of his tightly connecting feelings to moral performance in his depiction of Clarissa and loosely connecting feelings to moral performance in the other characters in the novel were disregarded in the rush to debase the sentimental into a popular value with little substantive and certainly no moral meaning. Clarissa is intended to be as much a representation of the innate moral sentiments in their ideal form as is Sophia. Having a sense of normative realism in these matters similar to Fielding's, Richardson grants that the nature of most human beings is mixed. But, like Fielding, he asserts in his main character an ideal of goodness in which goodness is defined as the innate moral sentiments writ large. Having decided that ideal goodness can best be dramatized when it is the seeming victim of absolute viciousness, Richardson's drama is the holocaust writ small. Lovelace is Clarissa's necessary antagonist and fate, then, and Clarissa's insufficient prudence is not only a device of characterization to propel her tragedy but also a negative measure of how true she is to her feelings. Though being true to her feelings may create serious worldly problems for her, such truthfulness cannot get her into trouble with God, whose bosom is her destination. Richardson's Clarissa, Fielding's Sophia, Dickens' Little Nell, and Thackeray's Amelia Sedley are cut from the same cloth of philosophical sentimentality. Whereas Fielding and Thackeray find comedic resolutions for the ideal in conflict with the flawed human community, Richardson and Dickens hear the angelic voices of a heavenly community singing a tragic chorus of the resolution that comes only in death.

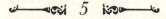 5

The distinction between sentimentality as an expression of the doctrine of the moral sentiments and sensibility as a register of the capacity to respond to external stimuli needs to be emphasized. Sentimentality is the possession of innate moral sentiments; sensibility is a state of psychological-physical responsiveness. The latter concept led in the second half of the eighteenth century and in the Romantic movement to portraits of the artist in which the defining characteristic is intense sensibility. Henry Mackenzie's *The Man of Feeling* (1771) embodies in its fragmentary form the "soft sense of the mind," a mind whose sensibility is so keen that it cannot tolerate the structures of literature or life. Its main characters are in retreat from life even before they have encountered it, convinced that they must flee from both experience and art. The "man of feeling" is a Romantic in embryo, contributing to and becoming absorbed into the Romantic fascination with the "numbness unto death" that may result from the man of keen sensibility dealing with the ordinary things of this world. Neither the moral philosophers nor the doctrine of the moral sentiments advocates retreat from experience and community, though not all the Romantic poets do either. Wordsworth, the Romantic poet most influenced by moral philosophy, favors the growth of the artist into community and into the service of "the still sad music of humanity."

Mackenzie did not offer the Victorians the attractive moral paradigms that Fielding and Richardson did, and though the Romantic influence was powerful throughout the nineteenth century, it was just that aspect of Romanticism, its glorification of sensibility, with which the Victorians felt most uncomfortable. Mackenzie contributed to the Romantic belief that the feelings are the source of joy rather than goodness. And, just as goodness has its necessary antinomy in evil, so too joy has its in pain. Mackenzie anticipated the depiction, in Keats's and Coleridge's poetry especially, of the feelings alternating between joy and misery, with the assurance that all joy irreversibly leads to isolation, alienation, and emotional numbness. The Victorians preferred "sense" to "sensibility," pursuing ideals to counterbalance the mixed nature of reality and intent on confirming community values as best they could. They were attracted to sentimentality as a moral and communal ideal rather than to sensibility which promoted separation and withdrawal. Mackenzie's reputation, inseparable from his depiction of "the man of feeling," survived with some dignity and respect into the Victorian period. But, though Dickens owned a set of Mackenzie's complete works, *The Man of Feeling* had lost most of its relevance by the Victorian years. In contrast, Goldsmith's *The Vicar of Wakefield* (1766) became for the Victorians the bible of moral sentiment. Its pastoral depiction of the triumph of innate goodness shaped and reinforced Victorian sentimentality. Whatever the attraction to modern readers of the thesis that the novel satirizes the optimistic visions of Dr. Primrose, Goldsmith's contemporaries and his Victorian admirers would have been stunned by the absurdity of such an interpretation.[18] "No book upon record," John Forster claimed in his influential biography of Goldsmith, "has obtained a wider popularity and none is more likely to endure"; for "good predominant over evil, is briefly the purpose and moral of the story . . . which sets before us, with such blended grandeur, simplicity, and pathos, the Christian heroism of the loving father, and forgiving ambassador of God to man."[19] To the Victorians, Dr. Primrose seemed a paragon of virtue whose adventures exemplify the good heart and the moral sentiments, and to see virtue was not only to admire but to love it.

Goldsmith's is a skeletal imagination, without the flesh of human fullness. But it is precisely this paradigmatic quality, this bare-boned presentation of grandeur in terms of the innate moral sentiments, that elevated *The Vicar of Wakefield* into its special position among the Victorians. That all humankind, even hardened criminals, had hearts that could be moved, innate moral responses that could be tapped, by the message of Christian love was a stirring reaffirmation of what many Victorians needed to believe. And the messenger was inseparable from the message. The Victorians loved *The Vicar of Wakefield*. It was a book that gave them moral "pleasure," a sermon in fiction that touched their hearts with the truth of its moral philosophy, uncomplicated by the larger canvas that the dialectic between the ideal and the real imposed on Goldsmith's predecessors. It seemed a version of *Joseph Andrews* with Parson Adams as the main character and without the complicating themes of Joseph's story. Everyone, Goldsmith claims, has the potential for the awakening of the moral sentiments, which are the prime constituent of human nature, given to us by a Universal Maker whose sectarian limitation as a Christian god does not prevent his smiling on all humankind.

Though Primrose, like Parson Adams, has his human imperfections, they are the source of comedy rather than satire, and *The Vicar of Wakefield* depends, as does *Joseph Andrews*, on the resolutions of comedy in which no expression of the moral sentiments can be too strong or too frequent. Even the occasional parodying of the language of popular sentimentality is gently put to the service of affirming the moral sentiments. Goldsmith, like Dickens, Thackeray, and Carlyle, was alert to the potential for the exploitation of sentiment in which people "*pay* you by *feeling*," a phrase from Boswell's *Life of Johnson* that Forster quotes in his *Life of Goldsmith*.[20] But Goldsmith and his Victorian advocates unequivocally rejected the self-protectiveness and the cynicism that deny that the moral sentiments are the basic constituent of human nature because there are many who abuse the language and the power of the moral sentiments for self-serving ends.

Victorian sentimentality inherited from eighteenth-century moral philosophy a strong anti-sectarian, though not anti-Christian, commitment. Strongly anti-Puritanical, it was antagonistic to Protestant fundamentalism, to the gloomy straitjacket of religious literalism. Within dissent, enthusiasm, religion as an experience of the feelings rather than of the intellect, flourished. Eighteenth- and nineteenth-century evangelicalism emphasized the religion of the heart. But it was part of a vision of human nature that credited God's grace rather than innate human qualities for religious conversion and moral performance. Human beings needed to make themselves as open and as responsive to God's grace as possible, but responsiveness to other stimuli, whether moral, aesthetic, or sensual, implied at best a failure of concentration on the main chance, at worst an improper if not corrupt attention to all those things that are not God. The Romantic poets directed the heart away from grace toward the self-sufficiency of the imagination. The Victorian novelists directed the heart back in upon its own high resources, the innate moral sentiments. And, since Dickens and his Victorian contemporaries were perplexed about the source of the moral sentiments and unable to explain in religious or other terms why some people have stronger moral sentiments than others, the evangelicals responded to Dickens with a grudging admission that he was of God's party without knowing it.

Dickens was, like Thackeray, purposely and deeply anti-Puritanical, which was both a particularized bias and an expression of his general disinterest in theological schemes.

Human nature fascinated him. Still, all his efforts to explain human nature in terms that relate individual performance to some cosmic scheme faltered from the beginning and failed in the end. To some degree, his sentimentality is inherent in his anti-Puritanism, but to a greater degree his sentimentality is the result of the deep satisfaction as well as the occasional perplexity he derived from defining human nature in the terms of eighteenth-century moral philosophy. More than any other great writer in the British tradition, Dickens has been accused of being pejoratively "sentimental" with little regard either for what such expressions of "sentiment" meant to him and his contemporaries or for the philosophical tradition that argued that the sentiments were inherently moral.

Victorian sentimentality was central to the attempt of British literature and philosophy in the first half of the nineteenth century to defend the value of the ideal against the increasingly powerful forces of philosophical realism, which claimed that the ideal has no place either in life or in literature.[21] Such realism represented the growing tendency in post-Renaissance European culture to conceive of human nature as basically flawed, unredeemed and unlikely to be redeemed by transcendent forces, the product of biology and social conditioning rather than of spirit and will, and best depicted within the confines of the permanent "prison-house" of everyday experience. Of course, the idealism associated with Plato and the belief in human perfectibility as a transcendent phenomenon made constant counterattacks, of which Victorian sentimentality was one. The counterattackers recognized the difficulty of resisting what they felt to be the demeaning view of human nature and human potential that ordinary modern experience seemed to support, and that the traditional doctrine of the fall had anticipated. The Bible itself could be seen as a stage in the development of philosophical realism in Western culture. As we move further away from Eden into history, the moral ideal becomes less a part of our daily lives and inappropriate to depictions, especially in the novel, of the truths of daily existence.

For the Victorians, the truths of philosophical and literary realism were disturbing ones. The fall from ideal epic proportions, if not of the body then of the heart, to human size and deflationary details needed to be resisted, both the act of falling itself and the even more dangerous belief that the fall had already occurred. The mock heroic of Pope and Fielding, the Manichaean conflict of *Clarissa*, the sardonic manipulations of human size from Swift to Louis Carroll, Blake's depiction of the fall of godlike man into constricting smallness, Thackeray's novel whose subtitle declares that it is without a hero, and Dickens' creation of ideal embodiments of the moral sentiments from Little Nell to Little Dorrit express how powerful and how difficult to resist the non-idealistic view of human nature had become. The doctrine of the moral sentiments was a key weapon against the elimination of the moral ideal, and Victorian sentimentality was a late, occasionally shrill stage in the rear-guard action to defend human nature from further devaluation.

Are You Sentimental?

⌇⸺⟡ *1* ⟡⸻⌇

When considering in the autumn of 1844 the subject of his new Christmas book, Charles Dickens was "all eagerness to write a story about the length of that most delightful of all stories, *The Vicar of Wakefield*." Goldsmith's novel, Dickens believed, had "done more good in the world and instructed more kinds of people in virtue, than any other fiction ever written."[1] Actually, Dickens had declared himself an eponymous child of Goldsmith from the moment of his first appearance in print, taking as his pseudonym Boz, a humorous mispronunciation of the name of Dr. Primrose's son, after whom Dickens had nicknamed his younger brother. *The Vicar of Wakefield*, which he knew even more intimately than he knew Fielding's and Richardson's novels, runs like a leitmotif through his fiction and, as did *Joseph Andrews, Tom Jones, Roderick Random, Humphry Clinker*, and *Clarissa*, influenced significantly his assumptions about human nature and the moral sentiments. Echoes of the Vicar sound from Pickwick to Crisparkle. Primrose is a constituent of all Dickens' portraits of benevolence, as well as of the vision of the healthy, active pastor or shepherd of the flock of humanity. Primrose's belief in the universal potential for moral reformation through an appeal to the moral sentiments underlies many of Dickens' efforts to depict moral rebirth, such as that of Eugene Wrayburn in *Our Mutual Friend*. Like Goldsmith's, Dickens' conviction that novels are vehicles, among other things, for teaching virtue, and that the moral sentiments are the source of virtuous actions, pervades his fiction.

But Goldsmith's influence is only one element in Dickens' transformation of the doctrine of the moral sentiments, with its nonsectarian Christian values, into sentimentality. In the channels of transmission, Fielding and Richardson also play a major role, especially in Dickens' commitment to creating ideal characters who are embodiments of the innate moral sentiments. Little Nell, Esther Summerson, and Little Dorrit, for example, are idealized representations in the mold of Sophia and Clarissa, embodiments of Dickens' belief in the moral sentiments, part of his effort to depict absolute ideals in a mixed world. Fielding claimed that "the Vices to be found" in *Joseph Andrews* "are rather the accidental Consequences of some human Frailty or Foible, than causes habitually existing in the Mind."[2] Though Dickens' sense of how deeply human flaws descend into the bedrock of "Mind" is more acute than Fielding's, his depiction of pure or absolutely good minds or hearts bears witness to his belief that idealized representations of the moral sentiments are an essential function of fiction. Modern dissatisfaction with such characters as Little Nell, Esther Summerson, and Little Dorrit evaluates them against a standard derived from the very anti-idealistic tradition and its devaluation of human nature that Dickens energetically opposed. For example, Dickens' depiction of the death of Little Nell, modeled on Richardson's depiction of the protracted death of Clarissa, assumes that both author and audience will respond to their shared moral sentiments with a depth of feeling that will validate the artistry of the dramatization as a moral force for individual rebirth and for communal health. The suppression of the innate moral sentiments Dickens believed responsible for much of the corruption of Victorian culture, including the perversion of the free play of the imagination that he depicts in *Hard Times*.

The power of the moral sentiments is so great, Dickens implies, that their condemnation as "sentimentality," in the pejorative modern sense, is a frightened defense against its demands. Indeed, the tears of sentimentality can dissolve the barrier that destructive individual and social pressures have erected to prevent the free expression of feeling. The Victorian "sentimentalists" believed that the alienating and dehumanizing pressures and structures of modern culture, all of them dry-eyed exponents of misery and suppression, are more and more separating human beings from their natural sentiments, and that the desire to repossess them is widespread even if dormant. The novelist's purpose, among others, is to awaken that desire and to help it fulfill its needs. A formalist aesthetic, then, is meaningless to Dickens because it values structure more than feeling. Though Dickens' aesthetic sense is reasonably well developed and his craftsmanship of the highest order, dramatizations such as the death of Little Nell must have seemed to him self-justifying, appealing to a higher tribunal than an aesthetic one.

⋇————⊰⊱ 2 ⊰⊱————⋇

The Romantic poet whom Dickens read closely and who most influenced him is Wordsworth. The "Lake Poet's" fascination with sentiment made him a pervasive presence among the Victorians. The "thoughts that do often lie too deep for tears" frequently surfaced into tearful expression in a vast Victorian literature and ideology of feeling that embraced, on the one hand, Mrs. Felicia Hemans and the ever-popular sentimental annuals and, on the other, John Stuart Mill's claim in his *Autobiography* (1873) that Wordsworth's poetry of feeling provided therapy to cure emotional deadness. As the Victorian years progressed, Wordsworth became a good gray ghost, a warmly familiar patriarchal embodiment of the value of the sentiments. Wordsworth helped to legitimize sentimentality for the Victorians. As Matthew Arnold remarked in "Memorial Verses," "he spoke, and loosed our heart in tears."

For Dickens, Wordsworth's glorification of the sentiments was sufficiently Christian to allay the possibility that a doctrine that advocated the primacy of the feelings might be thought of as potentially pagan. Excesses of the heart needed to be sharply distinguished from excesses of the body, Wordsworth needed to be distinguished from Swinburne, Christian liberalism from Romantic paganism. A safer poet for the Victorians than Byron, Keats, Shelley, or even Coleridge, Wordsworth's regard for the healing nature of feeling had its origin in the same belief in the moral sentiments and in the same view of human nature that Dickens and many Victorians held. "Lucy Gray," "Tintern Abbey," and "Expostulation and Reply" advocate the moral sentiments, and the poet of *The Prelude* believes in a congruence between the mind of man and the mind of the universe which can be apprehended only through the feelings. The poet can see moral patterns in the external world of nature because those moral patterns exist within him, and the act of seeing is a leap of comprehension made by the feelings. Wordsworth particularly attracted the Victorians by his combination of modernity and conservatism, by his transformation of eighteenth-century benevolent and optimistic beliefs into what Keats calls the "holiness of the heart's affections" and the moral nature of feeling into a language that expressed the nineteenth-century democratic ethos.

Frequent allusions and references to Wordsworth and his poetry in Dickens' letters and conversations testify to his familiarity with Wordsworth's "genius" from the beginning of the novelist's career. During the years he was at work on *Oliver Twist, Nicholas Nickleby,* and *Old Curiosity Shop,* Dickens owned the six-volume 1836 edition of Wordsworth's *Poems,* which was among the first set of books he purchased. When he dined with Wordsworth's son in 1839, he thought him "decidedly lumpish. Copyrights need be hereditary," he remarked, unwittingly anticipating his relationship with his own children, "for genius isn't."[3] He had no doubt about Wordsworth's genius, and he found in Wordsworth's poetry a model for and a confirmation of his own beliefs about human nature, the moral sentiments, and the role of the sentiments in literature. Dickens did not read the Wordsworth of *The Prelude,* who saw within external nature the potential for dark passions as well as for bright benevolence, and by and large he kept clear of Wordsworth's emphasis on the healing powers of landscape, though he had no particular argument with the view Wordsworth popularized of the rural world as a healthy antidote to urban ugliness and corruption. The pastoral landscapes of *Old Curiosity Shop* are one element in Dickens' dramatization of the traditional opposition between the country and the city, derived partly from eighteenth-century fiction and partly from Wordsworth.

Dickens was not attracted by Wordsworth's emphasis on the healing powers of nature because he believed that the crucial conflicts of modern culture, between the natural and the unnatural, between innate goodness and a hostile environment, take place within the city's walls, and that therefore the cure must come from within the self and be enacted within the urban environment. Nature is at best a refuge in which to hide and even to die, as do Little Nell and Betty Higden. But Dickens' reading of Wordsworth did help direct his attention to the sentiments as the source of moral feeling. He commented a half year before he began writing *Old Curiosity Shop* that "We Are Seven" is "one of the most striking examples" of Wordsworth's "genius," and the "simple Child" of the poem contributed to his portrait of Little Nell. The poem was still in his mind in 1842 when in a lighthearted reference he revealed how profound a part of his consciousness it had become. In *Old Curiosity Shop*, Dickens insists, as do Richardson in *Clarissa* and Wordsworth in "We Are Seven," that the faith of the feeling heart whose sentiments are moral can embrace dying as an ideal against which to measure the limitations of life and criticize those who prefer a corrupt life to an idealized death.[4] Echoing a poem by Wordsworth that he had read closely, Dickens asserted that "there *are* thoughts, you know, that lie too deep for words."[5] The purposeful misquotation manifests Dickens' awareness of the limitations of language in expressing feeling. But in *Old Curiosity Shop* and elsewhere, Dickens strove for a dramatic rendition of the sentiments (Wordsworth's "thoughts") that would bring to the visible surface that which often seems too deeply buried for effective expression.

Unlike Matthew Arnold, Dickens believed "sentiment" representable, a prominent if not the major constituent of his art. As a novelist, he did not feel bound by the restrictions of realistic characterization. On the contrary, he assumed that the moral ideal can represent the reality of the moral sentiments which "realism" tends to deny. The language of the moral sentiments can express that which the other vocabularies available to it at best only hint at and at worst disavow. Though Dickens misquotes the final line of Wordsworth's

"Ode: Intimations of Immortality on Recollections from Early Childhood" by substituting "words" for "tears," Dickens' actual practice restores the "tears." In *Old Curiosity Shop*, he affirms the Victorian belief that a wet face is not an embarrassment. Tears are an effective expression and communication of moral feeling.

Some of Dickens' contemporaries recognized the similarities between Dickens and Wordsworth, particularly influences and conjunctions of the sort that occur in "We Are Seven" and *Old Curiosity Shop*. Richard Henry Horne in *The New Spirit of the Age* (1844) favorably compared the accidental passages of blank verse in *Old Curiosity Shop* with "the best passages in Wordsworth, and thus, meeting on the common ground of a deeply truthful sentiment, the two most unlike men in the literature of the country are brought into the closest approximation."[6] Dickens' contemporaries thought his blank verse passages effective heightening of the language of sentiment, since "sentiment" itself belonged to the ideal expression of innate human nature. That nature, under constant attack from changing perspectives in modern culture, needed as much reinforcement as possible. Wordsworth and Dickens, in Horne's view, shared the common ground of "a deeply truthful sentiment" that was even more important than other similarities, including their shared concern with the child and with the influence of childhood on the formation of the adult.

Dickens had less interest than Wordsworth in analyzing the patterns of feeling and more in dramatizing the situations that produced them. Naturally, Dickens tends to be more melodramatic than Wordsworth, who finds his drama in meditation rather than in action. The underlying belief in the importance of feeling defined as moral sentiment and the impossibility of excessive feeling, however, is similar. Dickens constantly dramatizes heightened feeling arising from crises of action, and elaborate set scenes, reminiscent of Clarissa's extended death, are less frequent in Dickens' fiction than the notoriety of a few such instances, such as Little Nell's death, would suggest. When Wordsworth creates dramatizations of action, as in the death of Lucy Gray and the poverty of Alice Fell, he also effectively dramatizes heightened feelings. And the narrative thrust of Wordsworth's art in general, particularly within the ballad and the pastoral, is quite strong. But his art generally demands abstraction, not individuation, the search for and the dramatization of meditative patterns, for making sense out of sense data. Dickens prefers to dramatize the sense data and sensations *in extremis*—birth, death, marriage, separation, violence, communal rituals—individual, immediate responses to the passages of life. As selective as Wordsworth in what he chooses to see, Dickens desires to create the illusion that what he sees is more objectively real and less mediated through self-consciousness. The nature of his art demands a wider, more tactile canvas than Wordsworth's, whose subject is his own moral sentiments. The novelist's art is more indirect, the patterns of plot preceding the patterns of feeling. But Dickens and his novelistic contemporaries believed that the novel could be as effective an embodiment and communicator of the moral sentiments as poetry.

Much of the poetic literature of sentiment of the late eighteenth and early nineteenth century is neglected today, usually for sound aesthetic reasons, and the pressed hearts and flowers of Victorian keepsake books and annuals have been pressed into oblivion as well. With Wordsworth, the question of sentimentality rarely arises. With Dickens, it frequently does, partly because the sentimental poet in the Romantic tradition usually is granted the virtue of sincerity sufficient to his claims of feeling, whereas the nineteenth-century sentimental novelist, forced into a quasi-realistic straitjacket by the modern reader's expectations, often has his sincerity questioned. The modern allegation of sentimentality against the Victorians in general politely expresses a widespread feeling that Dickens and his contemporary writers were insincere. The novelist of sentiment is particularly reprehensible, for any novelist aware of his genre and in control of his craft should know that the assumptions about reality upon which the novel as a genre is based allow no place for an idealistic depiction of human nature. Such a depiction must be either insincere or in bad taste.

The charge of bad taste can be readily dismissed as irrelevant. "Taste" is a historical given, a standard derived from education, social position, and class structure. The standards that determine "taste" change as time passes. And what in art may be in good taste to one subgroup within our culture may be distasteful to another. Questions of taste ought best be suspended in the discussion of art, except in those instances of bad taste that are calculated by the artist to make a point. Bad taste is a matter of class rather than of aesthetics. Bad taste tends to be spontaneous, something one cannot help. Insincerity is purposeful, the manipulation of aesthetic materials for some self-serving, usually commercial, end. Henry Hallam in 1847 responded to the death of Dickens' Paul Dombey by remarking, "I am so hardened as to be unable to look on it in any light but pure business," suggesting that Dickens had manipulated the dramatic situation, eliciting from his readers feelings that he himself did not have in order to appeal to a debased popular taste for the purpose of selling more books.[7] R. H. Hutton in 1862 commented about both *Old Curiosity*

Shop and *Dombey and Son* that Dickens "spoons and stirs the subject of grief and death."[8] Like many Victorians who, from their superior class position, looked down on Dickens as a literary Bounderby, Hallam undoubtedly believed that Dickens frequently wrote in bad taste, spontaneously and unwittingly. That, however, for Hallam, was secondary and morally unimportant. Hallam, who felt certain that Dickens was consciously insincere, was probably more scrupulous than many of his contemporaries in distinguishing between bad taste and insincerity, and Victorian practice in general reveals the widespread assumption that one need not bother about such fine distinctions.

⚜ 3 ⚜

In his depiction of the deaths of Little Nell and Paul Dombey, Dickens dramatizes his belief in the innate moral sentiments and in sentimentality as morally instructive. "Yet nothing teacheth like death," one of Dickens' predecessors, whose works he owned, preached. William Dodd's widely read *Reflections on Death* (1763) is representative of hundreds of similar volumes whose depiction and evaluation of death the Victorians read. Dickens would have agreed with Dodd that

> it is too commonly found, that a familiarity with death, and a frequent recurrency of funerals, graces, and church-yards, serve to harden rather than humanize the mind, and deaden rather than excite those becoming reflections which such objects seem calculated to produce. Hence the physician enters, without the least emotion, the gloomy chambers of expiring life; the undertaker

handles, without concern, the clay-cold limbs; and the sexton whistles unappalled, while the spade casts forth from the earth the mingled bones and dust of his fellow creatures.[9]

In *Oliver Twist*, Dickens contrasts the easy familiarity and insensitivity toward death of Noah Claypool with Oliver's alertness to the inherent moral lessons in the coffin and the tomb. *Nicholas Nickleby, Barnaby Rudge*, and *Martin Chuzzlewit* also contain effective dramatizations of the moral significance of death, vivid embodiments of the Victorian concern with the potential devitalization of that powerful teacher of moral lessons and Christian virtues. To Dickens and his contemporaries, strong emotional response to death seemed more desirable than the all-too-common callousness, the kind of hardening of the feelings, that Dodd warns against. In a scene in *Reflections on Death*, which may have directly influenced Dickens' depiction of the death of Little Nell, Dodd dramatizes the death of a paragon of Christian virtue, a young mother who on her deathbed consoles her own parents, claiming that she is "wholly resigned" to God's will.

"I am on the brink of eternity, and now see clearly the importance of it—Remember, oh remember, that every thing in time is insignificant to the awful concerns of—" Eternity, she would have said; but her breath failed; she fainted a second time; and when all our labours to recover her, seemed just effectual, and she appeared returning to life, a deep sob alarmed us—and the lovely body was left untenanted by its immortal inhabitant! NOW SHE IS NUMBER'D AMONG THE CHILDREN OF GOD, AND HER LOT IS AMONG THE SAINTS.[10]

For her mourners, Nell provides a similar example of the lesson that death is a reminder to the living to allow their innate moral sentiments to flourish. To linger with expressive sentiment over the deathbeds or the graves of the departing or departed is to stand, even if prematurely, at the portals of paradise, being reminded that death is not only the mother of beauty but also that the moral sentiments that death evokes are the fountainhead of our feelings about the soul and about eternity. Dickens lingers for some time over Nell's deathbed, partly to affirm his commitment to Dodd's "important truth: The abuse of life proceeds from the forgetfulness of death." "Oh thank God, all who see it," Dickens writes of Paul Dombey's death, "for that older fashion yet, of Immortality! And look upon us, angels of young children, with Regards not quite estranged, when the swift river bears us to the ocean" (*DS*, chap. 16). Though some modern readers may be uncomfortable with the emotional intensity and the rhetoric with which Dickens describes such dyings, and may elevate discomfort and misunderstanding into an accusation of insincerity, Dickens is attempting purposely to arouse his readers' innate moral sentiments, reminding them that the more emotionally sensitive they are to death the more morally attentive they will be to the values of life. In the early stages of his career, Dickens felt optimistic that such dramatizations would stir the world's conscience as well as its fears. The suppressed and the exploited would benefit. He believed that fictional presentations of the deaths of children had extraordinary corrective potential. Such deaths appealed powerfully to the moral sentiments both because they seem against "nature" and "human nature" and because children are more vulnerable than adults. Intensely aware of children dead and dying, Dickens and many of his contemporaries thought it impossible to be excessively feeling or "sentimental" in any pejorative way about such losses. Attempts to curb the expression of such feeling denied human nature and human need.

⌐───◄◙≈ *4* ◙⌐───┐

In his influential biography of Goldsmith, John Forster quotes a passage from Boswell's *Life of Johnson*, the point of which Dickens, even more so because of his commitment to the moral sentiments, had well in mind.

> Boswell: "I have often blamed myself, sir, for not feeling for others as sensibly as many say they do." Johnson: "Sir, don't be duped by them anymore. You will find these very feeling people are not very ready to do you good. They pay you by feeling."[11]

The insincere expression of feeling and its exploitation for self-serving ends Dickens usually depicts as corrupt, a "paying" with counterfeit coin. For example, Edith Grainger's mother, "Cleopatra" Skewton, insincerely advocates the moral sentiments and the natural goodness of the feelings in an effort to expedite the selling of her daughter to the unnatural, unfeeling Mr. Dombey.

> "—about these cold conventionalities of manner that are observed in little things? Why are we not more natural? Dear me! With all those yearnings, and gushings, and impulsive throbbings that we have implanted in our souls, and which are so very charming, why are we not more natural?" Mr. Dombey said it was very true, very true. (*DS*, chap. 21)

51

Keenly aware of the danger of being duped by insincerity, Dickens gives some priority to communicating to his readers where he stands on such a matter. The widespread corruption of the sentiments and hardening of the feelings are destructive among other reasons because the hypocritical appeal to falsified feeling cannot always be distinguished from the expression of genuine feeling. Those who tarnish spiritual gold by manipulating feeling to obtain material gold Dickens satirizes and condemns. Johnson's reminder to Boswell that those who have moral sentiments demonstrate them in deed, a sounder currency than words, strikes forcefully at the heart of the danger, as the Victorians saw it, of disengaging moral feeling from moral performance. The pejorative use of the word "sentimentality" sometimes means just that: the degree of moral action is small in relation to the amount of expressed moral feeling, as if an implied promise to create consonance between feeling and action has not been fulfilled. The meditative poet, like Wordsworth, need only persuade that his feelings are sincere, appropriate in broad human terms to his means and his ends. The Victorian novelist, like Dickens, must always respond to the expectations of the novel as a genre and of his readers that expressions of feeling will be aligned with the settings and actions to which his narrators' and his characters' feelings relate. In a discussion of Arnold's poetry, Arthur Hugh Clough expressed the belief of many Victorians that fiction is superior to lyric and even dramatic poetry because it forces the artist always to relate feelings to performance.[12] Arnold himself confessed dissatisfaction with his early poetry precisely because it separated feeling from action, lacking the catharsis that only patterns of action can provide. Tennyson, in "Locksley Hall" and in *Maud*, compels the meditating, intensely "feeling" persona into social action, the theme in Arnold's "Rugby Chapel" of the marching band that leads us "on to the City of God."

To keep as narrow as possible the potential gap between moral feelings and moral acts has been, naturally, a long-standing concern in Western culture, frequently expressed in religion, philosophy, and literature, part of the traditional attempt to define human nature in moral terms. "Repentance, Prayer, and Charity" have been the sacred call within the Judaeo-Christian tradition for more than two thousand years. Like many of his contemporaries, Dickens believed that whereas previously such lack of consonance between feelings and actions could be isolated as rare examples, Victorian society manifested a reversal of the traditional ratio, both in individual and social terms. Now those rare instances of *consonance* between feelings and actions stood out as isolated instances. That frightening reality became for the first time the subject of the community's literature.

Numbness of feeling constantly confronts Keats and other Romantics as the inescapable result of the sensitive poet living in a world hostile to the imagination. The meditative odes of the Romantic tradition embody the poet's lyric dramatization of the pain and frustration arising from his awareness of the gap between his desire to express imaginatively the moral power of his feelings and his inability to do so. Such poems are psychodramas in which the poet is both victim and self-victimizer, and the highest aim of the performance is liberation from the closed circle of pain. Still, the performance is the artistic representation of the inner life, the representation of sensibility rather than moral sentiments, except in the case of Wordsworth, who emphasizes the consonance between moral feelings and moral acts, keeping the performance close to expressions of the moral pulse beat in the eighteenth-century sense, the "little, nameless, unremembered acts of kindness and of love," the growth and expression of the moral sentiments. Like many Victorians, Dickens takes Wordsworth as his moral and aesthetic mentor in his emphasis on the lack of consonance or separation between feelings and moral acts rather than between feelings and aesthetic or imaginative acts.

Though for Dickens the most important acts occur within the individual and private sphere, the origin of the gap between moral feeling and moral action is social. Like Carlyle, Thackeray, Tennyson, Browning, and George Eliot, Dickens focuses on the struggle of the private self to come to terms with the needs and the limitations of the private self. But the theater in which the conflict takes place is the public one. Dickens conceives of the external world as materially real (hardly something that we "half create" and "half perceive") and solidly there, independent of the mind of the artist. In that world, the gap between individual perception and external reality is minimal, at least in potential. There is no reason inherent in the substance of the world and in our process of perceiving it why we cannot see what is there, though some of Dickens' characters find it self-serving to see only what they want to. For Dickens, unlike most of the Romantics, the epistemological problem is minimal. The lack of consonance between feelings and acts is a moral and social problem more than it is and before it is a personal one.

One of the devices from the theory of moral sentiments that Dickens draws on is the man of Benevolence, who, in his idealized form, such as the Cheeryble brothers in *Nicholas Nickleby* and Mr. Brownlow in *Oliver Twist*, matches his innate moral sentiments with moral acts.[13] The Benevolent man is an epitome of moral sentiment. As a concept, Benevolence is a secularized development of Pauline Charity, the third

value in the apostolic trinity, which eighteenth-century latitudinarian religion and moral philosophy promoted as a hu-
manistic substitute. One of the many attempts to have Christian values without Christian dogma, it is an ethical concept
rather than a religious imperative, an attempt by eighteenth-
and nineteenth-century humanism to liberate itself from
theology.

Dickens' reading of eighteenth-century literature and his
pervasive latitudinarian sympathies attracted him to Benevolence as a device for depicting models of an idealized consonance between moral feeling and moral action. Though Dickens finds comic material in the problems that the Benevolent
man meets with in an imperfect world, particularly in *Pickwick Papers*, the Benevolent man exists, among other reasons,
to show how much better we and our world can be. As an
idealization of such consonance, the Benevolent man does
disappear from Dickens' fiction, at least in his easily recognized form, by the late 1840s, partly because the Benevolent
man provides assistance to a type of character whom Dickens
came to believe must self-reliantly struggle to determine his
own fate, partly because the Benevolent man has *a priori* the
means to manifest his Benevolence, whereas Dickens became
concerned with exploring the questionable sources of such
wealth. In addition, Benevolence is always embodied in a
male figure of the kind who, for biographical reasons, particularly his relationship with his own father, Dickens became
anxious and doubtful about. There are no idealized Benevolent men in Dickens' fiction after John Jarndyce in *Bleak
House*, and Jarndyce is substantially different from the Cheeryble brothers. Later characters, such as Wemmick, Boffin,
and Sleary, possess moral sentiments and charitable hearts
but not a commitment to Benevolence as a social program or

as a personal philosophy. The vision that compelled Dickens to create Abel Magwitch, the convict in *Great Expectations*, made it impossible for him to explore the problem of innate moral sentiment in complex characters within the limitations of the concepts and categories of Benevolence. Among other things, it became clear to Dickens that Benevolence oversimplified the social context and the possibilities of widespread remediation to the extent that it damaged the chances of other approaches. Under the guise of private charity, it had become a self-serving substitute for public responsibility. Still, Dickens' initial attraction to Benevolence, to the good father as an informal social institution, served him well in his early fiction.

〜───✦ 5 ✦───〜

Neither the *Oxford English Dictionary* nor any other authority has done better than Nicodemus Boffin in defining sentimentality, particularly the broad implications the word had for Dickens and many of his contemporaries. In *Our Mutual Friend*, Sophronia and Alfred Lammle, who have swindled one another into an unprofitable marriage, attempt to deceive and swindle for profit Georgiana Podsnap and the Boffins, but they are unmasked by Boffin.

> "Mr. and Mrs. Boffin," said Mrs. Lammle . . . "there are not many people, I think, who under the circumstances, would have been so considerate and sparing as you have been to me just now. Do you care to be thanked?"
>
> "Thanks are always worth having," said Mrs. Boffin, in her ready good nature.

"Then thank you both."

"Sophronia," asked her husband, mockingly, "are you sentimental?"

"Well, well, my good sir," Mr. Boffin interposed, "it's a very good thing to think well of another person, and it's a very good thing to be thought well of by another person. Mrs. Lammle will be none the worse for it, if she is."(*OMF*, Book IV, chap. 2)

To be sentimental, Mr. Boffin proposes, is a very good thing, for the desire to be thought well of *by* others and to think well *of* others is a manifestation of the moral sentiments. Boffin apparently posits a Humean standard of motivation in such matters, based upon an irreducible value with which there is no point arguing since it is not a rational matter. In *The Theory of Moral Sentiments*, Adam Smith cogently expresses Boffin's underlying assumption: "Man naturally desires, not only to be loved, but to be lovely; or to be that thing which is the natural and proper object of love. . . . He dreads, not only blame, but blame-worthiness."[14] This innate dread is existential, a self-correcting aspect of the moral sentiments that provides the spur to the moral sentiments when they are laggard. Sophronia's dread of being thought less well of, being thought worthy of blame by Georgiana, her husband mockingly refers to as being "sentimental." But Sophronia's sentimentality is the sign of her possession of healthy, functioning moral sentiments.

Adam Smith makes no uncertain claim that "Nature, when she formed man for society, endowed him with an original desire to please, and an original aversion to offend his brethren. . . . She rendered their approbation most flattering and most agreeable to him for its own sake; and their disapprobation most mortifying and most offensive."[15] The eighteenth-century moral philosophers believed that Society is a reflection of Nature and that Society and human nature mutually contain and reinforce the moral values of Nature. The Romantic idea that the moral sentiments can be cultivated best in solitude would have been as unacceptable to the moral philosophers as it was to the Victorians. Without society, Smith asserted, man has "no mirror which can present" the moral sentiments to his view. "Bring him into society, and he is immediately provided with the mirror which he wanted before."[16] But the mirror of society in Dickens' world, like the mirror over the Veneerings' sideboard in *Our Mutual Friend*, does not reflect the moral sentiments nearly as clearly as do the less obscured, cleaner mirrors of eighteenth-century moral philosophy. In Dickens' fiction, the mirror of enlargement has become the mirror of grotesque distortion. And the once clear glass has been made partly opaque by a film of Victorian dirt and doubt. It can no longer provide an accurate reflection of the moral sentiments inherent in Nature and in human nature.

Like numbers of his contemporaries, Dickens was attracted by the possibility of substituting moral paradigms in literature for those once provided by the mirror of society. But that venture had high risks, particularly for a novelist trying to reach a wide public. Dickens' public demanded that his novels provide it with a substantial degree of confirmation of widely accepted values. The considerable extent to which Dickens purposely did not provide his audience with conventional assurances while still keeping their loyalty is one of the measures of his genius. Unlike his friend Wilkie Collins, whose *Woman in White* exceeded in popularity any of Dickens' novels, the older writer imposed moral paradigms on his fiction, challenging his public to discover a corrective mirror of itself. Dickens throughout is basically non-mimetic. His main interest is not in accurately representing society but in creating a social world within his fiction that accurately embodies the moral paradigms that he believes are innate within human nature, society, and all things that are Natural. Often such a non-mimetic artist depends on mythic constructs or invents them, as Blake does. Dickens, tied to the things of this visible world, was aware of running another risk, the risk of substituting a personal vision for mimesis and unnaturally amplifying the voice of the artist beyond seemliness and natural sound. For the substitution of a literary mirror for a social mirror compounds the potential blasphemy and hybris by substituting a secular text for what had once been the mission reserved for scripture.

In *Our Mutual Friend*, the Boffins function as a mirror of the moral sentiments into which other characters can look and against which they can measure themselves. Without education or social position, the Boffins glow with natural good spirits, the spontaneous expression of their innate moral sentiments. Boffin assumes, despite his experiences with greed and viciousness, that his own moral sentiments are similar to other people's, and that most people do feel good when they know that others think well of them and when they think well of others. "It's a very good thing," Boffin states flatly, for the individual and for society, a claim placed beyond any train of reasoning. This is not a matter for disputation; it precedes cognition; the intellect is irrelevant. We need not and we cannot explain in rational terms why people feel good in engaging in such transactions with the self and with other people. Like the moral philosophers, Boffin believes that the moral sentiments are pre-rationally there. "The approbation," Hume writes, "which then ensues, cannot be the work of the judgment, but of the heart; and is not a speculative proposition or affirmation, but an active feeling of sentiment."[17]

Sophronia's tears are the outward expression of her moral sentiments, a visible sign that she has not moved so far away from her human nature that she cannot return to her natural sentiments when called. No wonder, then, that Dickens and many of his contemporaries are not opposed to tears. "My behaviour before my fellow passengers was weak in the extreme," Dickens proudly wrote to Wilkie Collins, for, while reading one of Collins' stories on a railway journey, "I cried as much as you could possibly desire."[18] Tears themselves are often the visible sign of rediscovering or returning to our first natures, our best human natures, our moral sentiments. Sometimes they are testimony to our never having been separated from our "natural" selves.

Sophronia's return to her moral sentiments is brief, a visit with what might have been rather than with what is. Under the pressure of her husband's expectations, she quickly masters her "sentimental" response, a lifetime of conditioning having made her adept at manipulating and suppressing innate moral feeling. "She walked to the window, flinching under his angry stare, and turned round quite coldly." She reminds Alfred that they are to flee abroad to escape their debts. "There is no fear of my taking any sentiment with me. I should soon be eased of it, if I did. But it will be all left behind. It *is* all left behind." Sentiment, she recognizes, is an intolerable obstacle to Alfred's profession and their union. Sophronia still can feel its power; Alfred Lammle has so suppressed or destroyed his moral sentiments that for all intents and purposes, as far as Sophronia can tell, he has never had any. Sophronia's expression of her moral sentiments in her final meeting with Georgiana may be taken either as an anomaly never to be repeated or a demonstration that, no matter how battered or suppressed, those sentiments will always surface in appropriate circumstances. Sophronia, then, joins that category of fictional Victorian women who exist to demonstrate that the moral sentiments can never be eradicated, and that women, for better and for worse, find it more difficult than men to suppress their innate natures. Since the moral sentiments remain a vital part of Sophronia's nature, they have the potential to become active again. Dickens concludes the chapter by expelling both the Lammles from the Victorian community in a wry parody of the first couple expelled from paradise. "She passed out and he followed her. . . . They went down the long street. They walked arm in arm. . . . In turning the street corner they might have turned out of this world."

Like many of his contemporaries, Dickens desired to affirm the community as the touchstone from which the moral sentiments can be evoked and against which human performance can find its proper measure of approbation and disapprobation. But the task was a difficult, almost an impossible one. The Victorian community from which the Lammles have been expelled often appears to the sharp eye to be an inadequate, even an unnatural, representation of Nature and human nature. And the artist must either bend under the pressure of social values or, as increasingly became the case, stiffen and rebel. Ironically, the Lammles turned the same street corner of exile that was to become the point of exit, whether literally or metaphorically, for many artists for whom society had become unnatural. For the moral philosophers, society embodied the perfection of the creation. In Dickens' fiction, neither society nor the creation is unequivocally good, and the Lammles represent a deficiency or perversion of the moral

immediately afterward came the question, Who or what is the source of those innate qualities that in aggregate we call human nature? Dickens' wide range of character types dramatizes the problem. Esther Summerson, Sissy Jupe, and Little Dorrit are from birth representations of fully realized moral sentiment. They are models that others, like Arthur Clennam, Louisa Gradgrind, and Sidney Carton, may use as inspiration for their own moral rejuvenation, for the awakening of their latent moral sentiments. But characters like Jingle, Monk, Ralph Nickleby, Quilp, Carker, Heep, Orlick, and Silas Wegg have moral sentiments to such a negligible degree that they challenge the assumption that moral sentiment is an innate human quality, a basic constituent of human nature. Dickens partly confutes that challenge by creating some characters, particularly Mrs. Clennam, Sidney Carton, and Miss Havisham, who also seem initially to be without innate moral sentiments but who demonstrate in crisis that they do have them. There are, though, few such characters in Dickens' fiction, and in the case of Miss Havisham the petrifaction of her moral sentiments is the *effect* of some *cause*. In contrast, Little Nell's and Little Dorrit's fullness of virtue and Quilp's and Heep's moral vacuousness seem not to be the effect of some cause at all. They are *a priori* givens.

But *who* is the giver? And why given in those proportions? And to what degree are such "givens" of human nature influenced by the environment? Dickens' attempt to answer these questions in narrative takes its force from his repugnance at what seems to him to be "unnatural." His most explicit rhetoric on the topos, in *Dombey and Son* (chap. 47), derives from widespread eighteenth- and nineteenth-century discussions of *Nature* in which *natural* and *unnatural* are the key oppositions. The line of discussion reaches from Pope's *Essay on*

Man (1744) to John Stuart Mill's posthumously published "On Religion" (1874). Unlike Mill, Dickens had no talent for or interest in semantic analysis. He could not define Nature, the natural, and the unnatural in other than experiential terms. Like his eighteenth-century predecessors, he assumed that the universe has "eternal laws" which govern the visible and invisible totality called "Nature." With the loosest of theological implications, Nature is the creation of God. Affronts to the "eternal laws . . . of Nature," Dickens believed, make Nature outraged, for Nature is the repository and expression of normative positive values. All manipulations or distortions of Nature, as "God designed it," result in unnaturalness. All manipulations and distortions of human nature, as "God designed it," result in unnaturalness. Dickens' phrase, assigning responsibility to the deity, is a generic one, representing his disinterest in pursuing the ultimate source beyond a conventional formula. And he is not always consistent in his references to the determining power behind Nature. But he implies that he has no difficulty distinguishing the natural from the unnatural in human performance. To that process of discrimination, central to Dickens' art as a novelist, philosophical and theological analysis is irrelevant.

Dickens generally depicts the world of physical nature in traditional Romantic opposition to the artificial creations of humankind. Little Nell flees from London as from a center of darkness into a rural paradise. But the countryside is Edenic because of the absence of certain evils, not because of the presence of Edenic forms. Since it provides Nell the security in which to express her natural goodness, it is paradise enough. Betty Higden, in *Our Mutual Friend*, flees the fallen city so that she may die peacefully in natural surroundings. Lizzie Hexam, seeking refuge from her painful relationship with Eugene Wrayburn, joins a fraternal community of workers in the countryside. Such versions of Dickensian pastoral are imbued with vague religious overtones, for the god who has created the "eternal laws of . . . Nature" can be more readily communicated with when his stars are clearly visible, one of which shows Stephen Blackpool, in *Hard Times*, "where to find the God of the poor." But in Dickens' fiction, that God or any other God at best puts in a shadowy appearance in the world of physical nature and often is hardly there at all. At times that world of nature only mirrors the qualities of the character who moves in it. Montague Tigg turns the woodlands into a nightmare with his murderous mind. Rogue Riderhood and Bradley Headstone transform the bucolic valley of the Thames into a landscape of mutual doom.

Since Dickens is concerned with physical nature mainly as a vehicle for dramatizing human nature, he implies no general overview of "the nature of nature" in his novels. He never claims that the physical world is inherently good. Unlike Arnold, he believes neither that nature is remorselessly indifferent to human concerns nor that "Man must begin . . . where Nature ends."[19] Landscape is not a book in which to read theology or mysticism or the answers to ethical questions. Though, as in the opening passage of *Little Dorrit*, it is sometimes depicted in animated, even anthropomorphic terms, this is an imagistic device to establish that the life of landscape comes from the life of the human mind and the functioning of human nature. Even the magnificent description in *Little Dorrit* of the crossing of the Alps confines Alpine grandeur within the dimensions of human psychology. No supernatural light ever transforms Alpine peaks or English valleys.

Dickens' subject, like Fielding's, is human nature. In its idealized representation, in characters like Little Nell and Little Dorrit, human nature is synonymous with the moral sentiments. Dickens grants such characters, by virtue of the fullness of their moral sentiments, the intuitive power to recognize the moral sentiments in other people and to discriminate effectively between the "natural" and the "unnatural." But it is only the authorial narrator who can speculate on the larger issues involved. "Was Mr. Dombey's master-vice," writes Dickens,

> that ruled him so inexorably, an unnatural characteristic? It might be worth while sometimes, to inquire what Nature is, and how men work to change her, and whether, in the enforced distortions so produced, it is not natural to be unnatural? (*DS*, chap. 47)

In the dramatic passages that follow, Dickens claims that social misery is an unnatural creation for which man, not Nature, is responsible. The universe is not inherently structured so as to make unnaturalness inevitable. The human beings malformed by social exploitation are not inherently sinful. For what we inherit is the culmination of "a long train of nameless sins against the natural affections and repulsions of mankind." An "unnatural humanity" has so distorted its own human "Nature" that it creates such unnaturalness and self-servingly argues that it is natural. But that unnatural condition need not last, and

> not the less bright and blest would that day of regeneration be for rousing some who have never looked out upon the world of human life around them, to a knowledge of their own relation to it, and for making them acquainted with a perversion of nature in their own contracted sym-

pathies and estimates; as great, and yet as natural in its development when once begun, as the lowest degradation known. (*DS*, chap. 47)

But once having had the natural "sympathies" narrowed and the moral sentiments constricted, few ever expand them. Like nerve cells, they are difficult to regenerate. And "no such day ever dawned on Mr. Dombey, or his wife; and the course of each was taken."

Dickens, of course, creates a large community of unhappy children and miserable adults. Many of them have had their moral sentiments or "sympathies" narrowed by social brutality, the exploitation and perversion of human nature that he associates with the industrial revolution and class structure. The degree to which the moral sentiments have been deadened varies from instance to instance, and characters like Nancy, the prostitute in *Oliver Twist*, and Jo, the crossing-sweep in *Bleak House*, keep their moral sentiments sufficiently alive so that they capture not only our sympathy but also our admiration. Oliver, Nicholas, and Little Dorrit have such strength of moral sentiment, among other advantages, that social "unnaturalness," no matter how seemingly powerful, cannot affect their heart's core and make them into less than idealized embodiments of the moral sentiments. But a great many characters in Dickens' novels are neither embodiments of the residual power nor idealized representations of the moral sentiments. Though the moral sentiments apparently are a universal given of human nature, some characters reveal that theirs have been diminished or deadened into invisibility. Others have maintained their moral sentiments at a sufficient level of latency so as to be able to resurrect them and themselves—characters such as Scrooge, Martin Chuzzlewit, Sidney Carton, Louisa Gradgrind, Arthur Clennam, and Bella Wilfer.

Do Dickens' villains have moral sentiments? The logic inherent in his notion of Nature and human nature demands that we conclude that they do. But such an optimistic characterology provides a vision of universal redemption *in potentia* that the experience of reading Dickens' depictions of his villains denies. If we assume that characters like Quilp, Squeers, Carker, Orlick, and Riderhood are themselves the victims of environmental distortion rather than being inherently deficient in moral sentiments, then indeed Dickens' view of the source of such immoral performances strains credibility. Smike and Jo, victims of extreme social brutality, nevertheless retain sympathy and moral sentiment, whereas Quilp and Carker, who have had easier lives, show no trace of such feelings. Dickens' villains, like his idealized models, seem to have been born into the perfection of their extremes. As adults, they are without redeeming moral value. Is it, then, that individuals have been treated differently from the beginning, from conception—that we have not all begun, in Dickens' world, from the same starting point? Have we each been given at birth a distinctive, unchanging amount of moral sentiment? Or is moral sentiment to be thought of as a potential for moral response rather than as a measurable substance? Dickens' characters are so different from one another in the degree of moral sentiment they possess that environmental influence alone cannot reasonably account for the differences.

The logic of innate moral sentiments, from Shaftesbury to Dickens, implies that Carker and Quilp have begun the race from the same starting gate and with the same handicap as Amy Dorrit and Little Nell. But much in Dickens' presentation of his villains and in common sense denies this. His villains seem always to have been and always to be unredeemable. It is one of their great attractions. It is also a complicating, enriching element in his fiction, a drama of the elect and the damned, the chosen and the forsaken, being played out on the same stage on which there is also being performed an optimistic human comedy about the triumph of the moral sentiments. That Dickens permits the possibility that there are people who do not possess moral sentiment at all is, however, a darker element in his vision of the human condition than his conviction that environmental corruption creates unnaturalness.

The environmental explanation had great appeal for Dickens. As the area of potential corrigibility, it deserved and got much attention. Within limits, it worked effectively, permitting Dickens and his contemporaries to believe that the basic human situation could be substantially improved through social reform. But Dickens also recognized that environmental pressure accounted for only a limited number—the middle range, shall we say—of instances of human unnaturalness. Like many of his contemporaries outside the evangelical world, he feared that the population of those seemingly without the moral sentiments at all was large and growing. At times it does seem that Dickens hoped that the elimination of environmental abuses would allow more light to shine on the obscure, fuller range of problems. Then, perhaps, we would see that what appear to be unchangeable, innate givens of human nature are not so at all but are *also* the products of social conditioning, that we indeed all have equal potential at birth for having and expressing moral sentiments. The Quilps and Heeps and murderous Riderhoods of our culture then will be seen not to have to have been. It is not a hope, though, that

Dickens maintained or sustained in his fiction as a whole or even throughout any one novel.

In general, Dickens chooses to operate as if, since the dark elements cannot be resolved, the bright counterpoint needs constantly to be affirmed. He is hardly alone among Victorian writers in this regard. But he stands in the modern retrospect as the Victorian writer most energetic in demonstrating, even in his later novels, that human nature contains innate moral sentiments whose expression is the heart of moral feeling and the pulse beat of the novel as a literary form. He is never ambivalent about dramatizing the moral sentiments: the more sentimental in that sense the better. And he is never dubious, even when environmental deformation is at its ugliest, about the eventual triumph of the moral sentiments for the individual. Every Dickens novel has one or more characters whose innate goodness cannot be perverted or destroyed by hostile forces. Even *Great Expectations* presents Joe Gargery as an epitome of untutored and innate moral sentiment whom Pip eventually learns to accept as a model superior to all the alternatives he has tried throughout his pilgrimage. Carlyle, with a rather different definition of human nature, always found invigorating what he thought of as Dickens' moral "cheerfulness," as if the sheer energy and moral bravura of his belief in the moral sentiments was itself a fiction so admirable that it transcended the limitations of fiction. Dickens' fiction was in fact a rear-guard action that Carlyle could sympathize with without ever believing in, an attempt to express the hope that moral deadness and social dehumanization are not inevitable.

Paper Sorrows

Jane Frith, the daughter of the painter William Powell Frith, whom John Forster commissioned to do a portrait of Dickens, saw the famous novelist many times at parties. As a young woman, intent on becoming a writer, she found herself drawn to Dickens' readings, though she admired Dickens as a writer less than she did William Makepeace Thackeray.

> [I] went more than once to [Dickens'] celebrated read-ings, and I must confess that while Nancy's murder made me ill, it was so truly ghastly that I only went once; I "could not away with" the pathos of Little Nell and Paul Dombey, and while I have seen everyone in the hall in floods of tears, and furthermore noticed that Dickens himself could hardly bear up under the weight of the woes he was creating, I could not share the sentimen-tal wave, and could not hear that the pathos rang true. But then I fear I have not much sympathy with paper sorrows.[1]

Frith maintained a strong reserve about "paper sorrows," partly to assert her independence of the Dickens vogue, partly to affirm her belief that fiction could not afford to weaken the power of its moral idealizations by a sentimentality that pro-duced pathos without emphasizing its moral base. As a counter to Dickens' "paper sorrows," she advocated what she believed to be Thackeray's more realistic view of the human situation. Hovering between the lines of her contrast is the modern critical argument about mimesis in art. Should the novel attempt to represent the real world directly or indirectly? And how are we to recognize what is real in relation to individual and to universal experience? Much of Western literature, until the birth of the novel as a literary genre, focused on ideal, transcendental dimensions, the interaction between the physical and the spiritual, between man and God. Not until the eighteenth century did literature begin to place primary emphasis on the depiction of the physical, historical world in mimetic narratives. Traditionally, reality in literature did not inhere in fidelity to the material facts of daily life but rather to the representation of widely accepted beliefs about the moral and spiritual structure of the universe and the place of human beings in it.

Alert to such matters, the Victorians felt both the tension and the complexity of the problem: how to deal with the gap between their desire to affirm the moral ideal as the highest reality and the growing disbelief in the validity of any experience other than that based on the patterns of daily life and the evidence of the senses. The effort to maintain a consonance between the ideal and the real provides one of the constant tensions within Victorian literature, for it is a central cultural question, expressed not only in fiction and poetry but also in the expository discussions of Carlyle, Mill, Newman, and Ruskin. The novel's popularity as a literary genre reveals the closeness of the issue to the public consciousness, on the one hand because it was central to the two most admired novelists, Dickens and Thackeray, on the other hand because the popularity of novelists like Wilkie Collins attests to with what relief the public turned in large numbers to fiction that disregarded the problem. In fact, the culture as a whole was gradually dismissing the problem, either by a return to religious fundamentalism or by a materialist denial that the problem existed at all. The major novelists, Dickens, Thackeray, George Eliot, and Trollope, fought that dismissal.

Though Thackeray is more keenly self-conscious than Dickens that sentimentality may degenerate into "paper sorrows," he is just as much as Dickens a sentimentalist who believes that human beings have innate moral sentiments. The distancing voice of his ironic narrator may sometimes mislead modern readers. But his irony is a defense against the widespread attack on the moral sentiments rather than a weapon in its service. Alert to the unnatural, self-serving misuses in literature and in life of natural feeling, the moral sentiments, and sentimentality, Thackeray's narrators frequently use irony to alert his readers to hypocrisy and to affirm that genuine feelings are the source of moral performance.

Though in 1858 Dickens and Thackeray argued on a personal matter, Thackeray always acknowledged their common struggle to affirm the moral sentiments and the ideal. "There are creations of Mr. Dickens's," he wrote in 1853 for his American audience,

> which seem to me to rank as personal benefits; figures so delightful, that one feels happier and better for knowing them, as one does for being brought into the society of very good men and women. The atmosphere in which these people live is wholesome to breathe in; you feel that to be allowed to speak to them is a personal kindness; you come away better for your contact with them; your hands seems cleaner from having the privilege of shaking theirs. . . . I may quarrel with Mr. Dickens's art a thousand and a thousand times; I delight and wonder at his genius; I

recognize in it—I speak with awe and reverence—a commission from that Divine Beneficence, whose blessed task we know it will one day be to wipe every tear from every eye.[2]

Thackeray means his claim that Dickens had a commission from divinity to be taken seriously, if still somewhat metaphorically. The dramatization of moral ideals is a sacred task given to novelists whose duty it is to provide models of innate goodness, the "very good men and women" from whose company "you come away better." Thackeray hoped that his novels would provide a mirror of the full range of human nature in which each individual could find the moral images against which to evaluate himself. Though granting that God eventually wipes away all tears, Thackeray believed that one of the functions of art in fostering moral improvement is to loosen the tears of feeling whose source is the innate moral sentiments. Those tears are a necessary part of the moral life. Thackeray detests false tears ("one tires of a sentimentalist who is always pumping the tears from his eyes or your own").[3] But genuine "tears are sacred."

In his response to David Masson's review, "*Pendennis* and *Copperfield*: Thackeray and Dickens," Thackeray expressed his "quarrel with Mr. Dickens's art"

which I don't think represents Nature duly; for instance Micawber appears to me an exaggeration of a man, as his name is of a name. It is delightful and makes me laugh; but it is no more a real man than my friend Punch is: and in so far I protest against him . . . holding that the Art of Novels is to represent Nature: to convey as strongly as possible the sentiment of reality.[4]

Fortunately, his argument here for a more literal realism did not prevent him from creating characters who are also exaggerations, caricatures, and even sometimes semi-allegorical representations of vices and virtues. Though Thackeray sincerely believed his novels to be more realistic than Dickens', probably he exaggerated the degree of difference, partly for the advantage of distinguishing himself from Dickens. Nevertheless, he recognized that his own focus on moral paradigms and on the moral sentiments, as well as his definition of the novel as filling a "commission" from divinity, made the difference less important than would appear on first look. Thackeray does pay more attention than Dickens to verisimilitude, for while in Dickens' fiction "a coat is a coat and a poker is a poker," it is also an element in a psychological characterization. Thackeray, of course, depicts Nature much as Fielding does, a stable external environment fixed by the reliable vision of the objective author-narrator. Dickens animates and interiorizes Nature, projecting onto it the state of the nervous system of the character or narrator. To the extent, then, that Thackeray is more of a realist than Dickens, his realism inheres in style and narrative point of view rather than in a material view of life. Actually, Thackeray's definition of human nature is strikingly similar to Dickens'. He too subscribes to the doctrine of the moral sentiments and to an idealistic definition of human nature. And the role of the novelist is to oppose the corrupting influence of Victorian culture by deflationary methods that never obscure the ideal and affirm the eventual triumph of "Truth, the champion, shining and intrepid" (*EH*, chap. 4). Like Dickens, he believes that there is "Truth"—*the* "Truth." But the defense and affirmation of the "Truth" against formidable opposition challenges both art and consistency.

Thackeray, whose personal library contained most of the classics of the previous century, absorbed deeply the eighteenth-century literature and philosophy he read from childhood on. His letters and essays record the development of his feelings and ideas about his eighteenth-century legacy, part of the living culture that shaped him as a writer to the extent that his consciousness about his predecessors became an important subject for his own writings.[5]

In a favorable review of J. H. Burton's *Life and Correspondence of David Hume* (1846), revealing his familiarity with both Hume and Smith, Thackeray admitted his special admiration for Hume, who was "good-natured . . . , one of the most generous, simple, honest, and amiable of men." Some years later, in *The Newcomes* (1853), he created Mr. Binnie, "a disciple of David Hume (whom he admired more than any other mortal)."[6] "Very much pleased" with Hume's essays on moral philosophy, "not for the language but for the argument," he shared his friend Edward Fitzgerald's admiration of Pope . . . "more and more for his sense." And though Hume was "the most amiable & honest of heathens," his opposition to Christianity as a theological system did not at all undercut his value to Thackeray as a source of wisdom about nature and human nature.[7]

Behind Thackeray's depiction of the fallen community in *Vanity Fair* (1848) is less the Augustinian City of God than the city of social harmony of the eighteenth-century moral philosophers. Like Dickens, Thackeray drew on the eighteenth-century image of the mirror of Nature to dramatize the failure of Victorian society to provide a mirror that accurately represents nature and the natural. In *Vanity Fair* (chap. 42), the great glass over the mantel-piece, faced by the other great console glass at the opposite end of the room, increased and multiplied between them the brown Holland bag in which the chandelier hung; until you saw these brown Holland bags fading away in endless perspectives, and this apartment of Miss Osborne's seemed the centre of a system of drawing rooms.

The shifting, multiplied perspectives, making it difficult to distinguish the real from the unreal, signal the collapse of an objective and unitary social order into subjective illusions and mirror tricks. In this world, there is no stable mirror into which we can look for moral guidance, no "impartial spectator" among the characters to provide a representation of Nature against which to measure our own naturalness. The "system of drawing rooms" is an optical illusion, a manipulative deceit. Everything and everyone, except the narrator, is made unreliable by the optical distortions, and only the narrator-author, positioned partly outside the false "system," can serve as the "impartial spectator" for this world.[8] Without a trustworthy social mirror, the artist must look for the "centre" in himself.

Thackeray's fascination with eighteenth-century culture derived partly from his belief that it offered helpful models of a consonance between Nature, human nature, and society. When he chose to lecture in England and America on the English humorists of the eighteenth century, he had a didactic, moral purpose, similar to his purpose in *Vanity Fair*. The choices he made about which authors to focus on reflect his commitment to tackle directly the questions about human nature that his novels dramatize. To some extent, the effort is a self-serving corrective. Confident that "human nature" can be meaningfully described and defined, he felt the need to shape his Victorian audience by creating and fortifying between author and audience a common ground of literary experience. Without such a common ground, his own novels might be misunderstood, particularly the role of the ironic narrator. In fact, the subtitle of *Vanity Fair*, "A Novel Without A Hero," had prompted some readers to conclude that the author believed human beings incapable of moral performance, and that neither life nor literature permitted moral ideals. The charge of cynicism, even nihilism, had been raised, as if Thackeray's exposure of human weakness and social corruption meant that he believed human nature to be irredeemably nasty.

Thackeray also suffered the advantages and disadvantages of his serious reputation being founded mainly on *Vanity Fair*, his greatest critical success. Victorian opinion in general held that the voice of the narrator of that novel was the voice of the author. Though the assumption was not unfair, the misinterpretation of the narrator's irony made Thackeray the target of criticism to which he was particularly sensitive, because it contradicted his actual beliefs about human nature and the function of literature. Thackeray shared the widespread Victorian conviction that authorship is a moral responsibility, a public revelation of one's values for didactic purposes. And he emphasizes in *The English Humourists of the Eighteenth Century* (1853) that literary criticism is not as central a concern of the writer and his audience as are the extra-literary "truths" embodied in the author's works and in his biography. Literary criticism for Thackeray *is* biography. The moral core is indivisible, the life and the works coextensive. That moral core, or innate moral sentiment, is an exemplar around which the fruit of Victorian fiction, biography, and autobiography grows. It can be argued, indeed, that biography was the model for fiction from Richardson to Joyce. But it was particularly dominant in Victorian fictional and nonfictional prose, partly because the relationship between models in life and models in literature was being questioned and the traditional relationship cast into doubt. *Vanity Fair* dramatizes that doubt, though Thackeray never has the slightest intention of letting that doubt triumph. In his essays and fiction, he defends the moral sentiments as innate and sentimentality as a way of expressing them. And just as human beings reveal themselves both in action and in temperament in the register of each individual's prevailing tone, so too do literary works, whose moral record and tonal register are coextensive representations of their authors. To talk about one is to talk about the other. For Thackeray, all literature is autobiographical mimesis.

In the first chapter of *The English Humourists*, which is devoted to Swift, Thackeray remarks that

> the humorous writer professes to awaken and direct your love, your pity, your kindness—your scorn for untruth, pretension, imposture—your tenderness for the weak, the poor, the oppressed, the unhappy. To the best of his means and ability he comments on all the ordinary actions and passions of life almost. He takes upon himself to be the week-day preacher, so to speak. Accordingly, as he finds, and speaks, and feels the truth best, we regard him, esteem him—sometimes love him. And, as his business is to mark other people's lives and peculiarities, we moralize upon his life when he is gone—and yesterday's preacher becomes the text for today's sermon. (*EH*, chap. 1)

But who can "love" Swift even "sometimes?" The Victorians

desired to love those whom they admired, to believe that those worthy of admiration for whatever their achievement are also worthy of love. Swift, in Thackeray's view, loved neither himself nor others, for "he was always alone—alone and gnashing in the darkness, except when Stella's sweet smile came and shone upon him," that idealized Stella who in Thackeray's mind had the beneficent power of an Amelia Sedley, Laura Bell, or Little Dorrit. Though Thackeray had great respect for Swift's genius, he viewed him, as did Dickens, as a Hobbesian figure of darkness. Swift promoted a "gloomy" misanthropy that subverted moral conduct, denied the moral sentiments, and discharged the moral temperament from what Thackeray believed was its obligation to be hopeful.

> We view the world with our own eyes, each of us; and we make from within us the world we see. A weary heart gets no gladness out of sunshine; a selfish man is skeptical about friendship, as a man with no ear doesn't care for music. A frightful self-consciousness it must have been, which looked on mankind so darkly through those keen eyes of Swift. (*EH*, chap. 1)

Thackeray, of course, prefers "humourists" in the cheerful Horatian mode partly because he believes that a true awareness of our own innate moral sentiments and their potential gives cause for cheer.

Like Dickens, Thackeray is persistently anti-theological. In general, the evangelical temperament repels him. Also, he believes that the innate moral sentiments rather than spiritual grace are the source of individual and social happiness. His characters live in a world without God—a world in which personal goodness is superior to divine grace. The transcendental mechanism is completely unavailable to Thackeray. Like

Fielding, he has no sympathy for "Abraham's bosom" or heaven as a motive for action, a perceived reality, or a reasonable destination. He prefers not to deal with death, certainly not to linger over it, as if the disposition of human nature after death is more uninteresting, and certainly more troublesome, than it is in life. Usually in Thackeray's fiction death provides only an ironic coda to the moral conditions of the life that has ceased; it facilitates plots, not themes. And the eighteenth-century "humourists" whom Thackeray most admires use it in much the same way.

Richardson is notably absent from *The English Humourists*, who apparently qualify for inclusion either by being satiric like Swift or comedic like Fielding. Thackeray's distaste for Richardson mainly derives from his distaste for the tragic mode. It was the Richardson of *Clarissa* rather than of the comedic *Pamela* and *Sir Charles Grandison* that Thackeray and his contemporaries knew. The resolution of conflict through death and the tragic vision of life that such a strategy entails implied for the Victorians an unhappy disconsonance between the individual and society—an unhappiness Victorian tragic drama dealt with by emphasizing moral models in which tragic necessity is minimized and loss affirms rather than questions the society's basic values. Even the great Victorian Shakespeare revival, led by William Macready and Sheridan Knowles and strongly supported by Dickens and Forster, temporized with the conclusions of Shakespeare's major tragedies. Dickens' friend Charles Fechter became a popular Hamlet. Macready gave stunning performances as Lear, Othello, and Macbeth, Macbeth's destruction represented as a triumph of the moral norms that the Victorians could applaud. But the deaths of Lear, Othello, and Hamlet dramatized different aspects of the conflict between the individual and society and presented definitions of human nature that many Victorians found disturbing. Some desired that representations of death contain assurances that death will be crowned with the rewards of heaven or the punishments of hell. Others sought in the depiction of death affirmation of the victory of the moral sentiments in life. Since tragedy as a literary genre provided neither, the Victorians both embraced melodrama as their favorite dramatic form and Victorianized the classic tragedies.

Thackeray respected the widespread Victorian preference that literature please rather than distress. Pleasure derives from moral models and moral guidance, for "human nature," Thackeray writes, "is always pleased with the spectacle of innocence rescued by fidelity, purity, and courage."[9] In *Clarissa*, Richardson offered his readers no such pleasure, and his depiction of a society so alienated from these virtues that it destroys the one person who possesses them Thackeray found unhelpful and painful. For Thackeray, Clarissa's tragic end does not justify the intensity of her emotional life, sentimental in the pejorative sense that it dramatizes feelings that are not validated by a comedic resolution. Thackeray, who admires "benevolence, practical wisdom, and generous sympathy with mankind," does not find these qualities in Swift and Richardson, partly because of their darkness. He also does not find them in Sterne, whom he takes as his primary target, mainly because of what he believes to be Sterne's dishonesty about the feelings. Because Sterne substitutes self-conscious, false sensibility for sincere sentiment, Thackeray criticizes him for dishonest manipulation of the "sentimental faculties." His feelings are in the service of a performance rather than the performance being in the service of the moral sentiments.

How much was deliberate calculation and imposture—
how much was false sensibility—and how much true
feeling? . . . Some time since I was in the company of a
French actor, who began after dinner . . . to sing . . . a
sentimental ballad—it was so charmingly sung that it
touched all persons present, and especially the singer
himself, whose voice trembled, whose eyes filled with
emotion, and who was snivelling and weeping quite genuine tears by the time his own ditty was over. I suppose
Sterne has this artistical sensibility; he used to blubber
perpetually in his study, and finding his tears infectious,
and that they brought him a great popularity, he exer-
cised the lucrative gift of weeping. . . . I own I don't
value or respect much the cheap dribble of those foun-
tains. He fatigues me with his . . . uneasy appeals to my
. . . sentimental faculties. He is always looking in my
face, watching his effect . . . and imploring me: "See
what sensibility I have—own now that I'm very clever—
do cry now, you can't resist this." (*EH*, chap. 6)

A full discussion of Richardson is omitted from *The English
Humourists* because he writes in a mode that makes his omis-
sion sensible. He is, in effect, playing in a different league.
Sterne, Thackeray believes, is playing in the same league and
cheating. And his dishonesty is compounded by his indecency,
for "the foul satyr's eyes leer out of the leaves constantly. . . .
I think . . . of one who lives amongst us now and am grateful
for the innocent laughter and the sweet and unsullied page
which the author of *David Copperfield* gives to my children"
(*EH*, chap. 6).

There does exist between the lines of *The English Humour-*

ists a subtext that is less well-disposed to Dickens. Thackeray, in 1853, had no desire for either private or public conflict with his fellow novelist, even on seemingly impersonal aesthetic grounds. For the Victorians, though, aesthetic disagreements almost always had moral and personal implications. In his attack on Sterne, Thackeray did not distinguish aesthetic from moral matters and in general did not recognize any division between an author's works and his life. To be hypocritical in literature is to be a hypocritical person. To be thought a bad writer is a moral as well as an aesthetic judgment. Until the rupture between the two writers, in 1858, Thackeray strained to keep up good relations with Dickens.[10] Where he could praise, mainly in regard to moral purity and imaginative vividness, he always did. And for his depiction of the triumph of the moral sentiments, Dickens received Thackeray's uninhibited approval.

In practice, Dickens' sentimentality differed considerably from Thackeray's, and Thackeray, I suspect, struggled to find indirect ways to express, if he could not completely suppress, his sense of that. Describing in *The English Humourists* the differences between Fielding and Richardson, he implies that he has in mind his own differences with Dickens, concluding that "Richardson's sickening antipathy for Henry Fielding is quite as natural as the other's laughter and contempt at the sentimentalist." Thackeray, of course, identified himself with Fielding and Dickens with Richardson, though in the development of the comparison the similarities are neglected, the differences exaggerated. In basic philosophy, both pairs of writers are sentimentalists and idealists, believing in the moral sentiments as the key to moral action and human nature. But to Thackeray, the dark drama of *Old Curiosity Shop* must have seemed remarkably similar to the dark drama of

Clarissa. And Richardson and Dickens must have appeared to Thackeray masters of the same techniques, the philosophical base of which was sound but the manipulative powers of which were suspect. Dickens' debts to Richardson were considerable. Thackeray's sympathies were too closely aligned with Fielding to permit him to have approved of the Richardsonian element within Dickens' fiction and to prevent him from transferring the lines of opposition between the eighteenth-century novelists to his own frequent comparison of himself with his rival.

～──～～ 3 ～～──～

Thackeray makes clear in his essay on "Fielding's Works" and in his discussion of Fielding in *The English Humourists* that he believes in the theory of the moral sentiments and in the selective depiction in fiction of idealized models of human nature. His crucial text is Fielding's *Amelia* (1752), for "the picture of Amelia . . . is . . . the most beautiful and delicious description of a character [Thackeray means here the worth of her character rather than the manner in which she is described] that is to be found in any writer, not excepting Shakespeare."[11] Amelia Sedley in *Vanity Fair* and Laura Bell in *Pendennis* are probably meant to evoke the moral perfection of Fielding's Amelia whom Thackeray and many others believed to be a portrait of Fielding's deceased wife, just as Amelia in *Vanity Fair* is said to be derived from Thackeray's "memories of his wife." For Thackeray, life and literature are mutually enriched by being identified with one another; life provides the moral paradigms for literary portraits. But what is it that makes Fielding's Amelia "the most beautiful and delicious de-

85

scription of a character . . . found in any writer, not excepting
Shakespeare"? In Thackeray's eyes, Amelia embodies the
highest degree of virtue as innate moral sentiment that any human being can possess, so powerful in its absoluteness that it
cannot be corrupted or even undermined either by the pressures of environment or by other aspects of her own nature.
Uncontaminated by realism or by Puritan theology, her innate
moral sentiments define her essence. But she is neither angel
nor angelic. Her needs and inclinations are of this world; her
role is to demonstrate that worldly satisfactions are morally vi-
able on the highest level. Instinctively distinguishing right
from wrong, good from evil, life from death, she cannot be
other than true to her moral feelings.

Fielding's Amelia is a creation of moral philosophy. When
she expresses her heart-weariness at the failure of others to act
on their moral sentiments, she is reminded by Dr. Harrison
what "the nature of man is."

> "Indeed, my dear sir, I begin to grow entirely sick of
> it," cries Amelia: "for sure all mankind almost are vil-
> lains in their hearts."
>
> "Fie, child," cries the doctor. "Do not make a conclu-
> sion so much to the dishonour of the great Creator. The
> nature of man is far from being in itself evil; it abounds
> with benevolence, charity, and pity, coveting praise and
> honour, and shunning shame and disgrace. Bad educa-
> tion, bad habits, and bad customs, debauch our nature,
> and drive it headlong as it were into vice. The governors
> of the world, and I am afraid the priesthood, are answer-
> able for the badness of it."
>
> "You understand human nature to the bottom," an-
> swered Amelia; "and your mind is a treasury of all an-
> cient and modern learning." (*Amelia*, chap. 9)

This is also Thackeray's view of human nature. He prefers to believe in innate goodness rather than innate corruption. But, like Dickens, he also is baffled by first causes and occasionally is ambivalent about the role of environment. Are human beings always born with good natures? And why do some seem to have better natures than others? In Thackeray's fiction, the evidence pertaining to these matters is ambivalent, especially in regard to those characters who embody the mixed nature of human nature. The evidence from his nonfiction is considerably less ambivalent in its expository directness, the reductive knife of analysis cutting more sharply through the problems than do the novels, which are responding to the pressures of literary realism and the complexity of human experience. He again quotes Fielding's *Amelia* to make his point. For though "Mandeville hath represented human nature in a picture of the highest deformity," Bob Jones, "who can never be supposed to act from any motive of virtue or religion, since he constantly laughs at both," in "his conduct . . . demonstrates a degree of goodness" which proves that his "human nature" is innately moral. All he need do is act in consonance with how he feels, with his moral sentiments, for "all men act entirely from their passions" (*Amelia*, chap. 13). The same is true of William Dobbin, Amelia Sedley, and Laura Bell, and would be true for George Osborne, Pitt Crawley, and, I suppose, even Lord Steyne, if "bad education, bad habits, and bad customs" had not driven them "headlong as it were into vice. The governors of the world . . . are answerable for the badness of it."

Why, though, do the "governors of the world" govern badly? Greed? Pleasure? The satisfactions of power? To say that environment or "the governors of the world" are at fault means no more than that these human beings, whose natures are supposedly "moral," have been massively immoral in the past and continue to be so in the present in ways that subvert the natural goodness of large numbers of people. Like Dickens, Thackeray is baffled by the difficulty of harmonizing an ideal model of human nature with the existence of crime and nastiness. All he can do, in this regard, is to recognize the novelist's limitations. "He tries to give you," Thackeray writes of Fielding, "as far as he knows it, the whole truth about human nature: the good and evil of his characters are both practical."[12] Aware that we cannot fathom the origin or understand the mechanism of the distribution of elements within human nature, the novelist commits himself to a literary genre that places emphasis on depiction rather than on explanation. For the novelist, "good" and "evil" are of this world, practical matters that concern the community of mankind rather than the theories of philosophy or the topography of God. The practical reality that the novelist and his audience must absorb into their world view is that most people are neither very good nor very bad. But Thackeray believed that one of the functions of the novel is to remind us of the potential for the full recovery and expression of the moral sentiments as the dominant constituent of human nature. That some of his contemporaries thought of him as a misanthropic Swift bewildered him. The author of *Vanity Fair*

> has lately been described . . . as a . . . dreary misanthrope, who sees no good anywhere . . . and only miserable sinners round about him. So we are; so is every writer and every reader I ever heard of; so was every being who ever trod this earth, save One. I can't help telling the truth as I view it, and describing what I see . . . that truth must be told; that fault must be owned; that pardon must be prayed for; and that love reigns supreme over all.[13]

Outside religious myth no one is perfect, even Laura Bell, to whom Pendennis says, "I think for some of you there has been no fall" (*Pen*, chap. 3). Thackeray the satirist depicts our vices. Thackeray the humorist reminds us of our potential for virtue.

The humorist, though, must not overvalue human nature, though the degree of our distance from the ideal is a measure of our situation, not our potential. Thackeray's literary realism demands that he depict the mixed nature of human nature, the normative probabilities within the world of experience. Still, for Thackeray, normative probability takes its value from its interaction with the ideal, and it is the function of literature, in a secular age, to provide a moral mirror against which mankind can measure itself. But for the mirror to be corrective, it must be supportive, and to be supportive it must be good-humored. Good humor is a manifestation of the moral sentiments, and the appeal to the moral sentiments is an appeal to love of others, to the congruence between the needs of the individual and those of the community. Thackeray grants that worldly experience cannot prove that human nature is innately good. Only the evidence of the feelings demonstrates that. Do we not always want, Thackeray implies in the terms of eighteenth-century moral philosophy, to do the right thing, to do the good thing? Do we not know that we will *feel* good by doing good, that we have within us the capacity to get the highest pleasure from moral actions, separate from all considerations of religious tone and theological doctrine? It is, Thackeray concludes, the novelist's responsibility to deepen his audience's awareness of its innate pleasurable response to goodness and its innate hostility to evil. The highest level of authorial trust is moral, and the devices of sentimentality are among the most effective that an author has to fulfill his duty, the awakening and strengthening of our moral sentiments. "Accordingly, as he finds, and speaks, and feels the truth best, we regard him, esteem him—sometimes love him" (*EH*, chap. 1).

—✦—✦ *4* ✦—✦—

As an author, Thackeray would have liked to have been loved, as he felt Dickens was. But in this he did not succeed, in his own judgment, to any satisfactory extent. Readers like Jane Frith found his representations of idealism more attractive than Dickens'. But Thackeray knew that many of his readers thought his novels admirable for the very cautiousness of temper and tone that made their favorite author and his readers less susceptible to "the sentimental wave" than were Dickens and his. The "sentimental" author most loved by the Victorians, and with whom Thackeray felt a close sympathy, he reserved for the place of final emphasis in *The English Humourists*. Structurally, the misanthropic Swift was to be balanced by the "philanthropic" Goldsmith. Thackeray, like Dickens, believed that Goldsmith's optimism and "Good-nature" were the ultimate model for emulation. Goldsmith's moral sentiments seemed to the Victorians the same in life as in literature, the essence of human nature as morally good in its instinctive feelings, eliciting and returning love. "Who, of the millions whom he has amused, doesn't love him? . . . To be the most beloved of English writers, what a title that is for a man!" Thackeray approvingly quotes Sir Walter Scott's remark that "we read *The Vicar of Wakefield* in youth and in age—we return to it again and again, and bless the memory of an author who contrives so well to reconcile us to human nature" (*EH*, chap. 6).

Thackeray felt a close identification with Goldsmith, whose early struggles as a writer reminded him of his own before the success of *Vanity Fair*, for, "except in rare instances, a man is known in our profession, and esteemed as a skillful workman, years before the lucky hit which trebles his usual gains, and stamps him a popular author" (*EH*, chap. 6). Constantly evaluating himself in the mirror of Goldsmith, he sometimes found himself wanting, as a matter of temperament rather than message, and Thackeray gracefully conceded that Dickens had taken up in the popular affections the ground that Goldsmith had stood on. Like Dickens, Goldsmith was "merciful, gentle, generous, full of love and pity. . . . His benevolent spirit seems still to smile upon us: to do gentle kindness: to succor with sweet charity: to sooth, caress, and forgive" (*EH*, chap. 6). His own temperament Thackeray thought too self-conscious and controlled for such a range of good works, but he was capable of expressing his generosity, his moral feeling, and his self-deprecating good humor in a touchingly personal way, conceding that Dickens is closer to Goldsmith than he.

All children ought to love him. I know two that do, and read his books ten times for once that they peruse the dismal preachments of their father. I know one who, when she is happy, reads Nicholas Nickleby; when she is unhappy, reads Nicholas Nickleby; when she is in bed, reads Nicholas Nickleby; when she has nothing to do, reads Nicholas Nickleby; and when she has finished the book, reads Nicholas Nickleby over again. This candid young critic, at ten years of age, said: "I like Mr. Dickens's books much better than yours, papa;" and frequently expressed her desire that the latter author should write a book like Mr. Dickens's books. Who can? Every man must say his own thoughts in his own voice, in his own way; lucky is he who has such a charming gift of nature as this, which brings all the children in the world trooping to him, and being fond of him.[14]

It is at the conclusion of *The English Humourists* that Thackeray most strongly avows his belief in the view of human nature and human society expressed by the eighteenth-century moral philosophers. For "the great world, the aggregate experience, has its good sense, as it has its good humour. . . . It gives you a fair place and fair play." All seeming malevolence is produced by "mistake, and not ill will" (*EH*, chap. 6). The faults of this world are neither theological nor purposeful, and they are not inherent in human nature or in society. Though his acceptance of the inevitability of mistakes has sometimes been thought cynicism, leading some readers to conclude that his sentimental characters and situations are to be taken ironically, Thackeray never satirizes fundamental goodness. He is committed to the moral sentiments as the essence of human nature and to a view of society in which "the great world, the aggregate experience, has its good sense, as it has its good humour." Sometimes, perhaps, he does not sufficiently emphasize the "good sense" and "good humour" to make his theme explicitly clear. But that William Dobbin and Amelia Sedley will not be perfectly happy forever after is not an expression of Thackerayan cynicism but his good-humored recognition that this is an imperfect world which literature must recognize while at the same time attempting to improve. Yet even amidst the corruptions of *Vanity Fair*, as in *Rape of the Lock*, good sense and good humour ultimately do prevail, providing idealized models against which we can evaluate our own moral sentiments. In that sense, Thackeray is as sentimental and as idealistic as Dickens, and there are no dark corners in *his* fiction that challenge the distinction between "mistakes" and "ill will."

Since all sorrows in literature are "paper sorrows," Jane Frith's distinction between Dickens and Thackeray misses the fundamental similarity between them. Thackeray humorously satirizes "Mes larmes" when they are false; he reveres them deeply when they are sincere. Then they are "sacred." So too does Dickens, for natural tears water the moral sentiments while unnatural expressions of feeling mock and pervert the true nature of human nature. Though it might be possible to construct a barometer that would measure comparatively the amount of sentimental moisture in Dickens' and Thackeray's works, the basic premise of both is sentimental in the philosophical sense. Like Dickens, Thackeray believes that human nature is innately moral, and that moral action is the result of moral feeling.

The Water Works

❧ ——◄❂❧ *1* ❧❂►—— ❧

Thackeray hoped that secular literature might replace society and scripture in serving to provide the models against which to measure our moral sentiments. As a conscious sentimentalist, who believed that such sentiments are an innate part of human nature, he appreciated the challenge that such a responsibility entails. Unlike Dickens, he was particularly conscious of false sentimentality, partly because he sensed how damaging it is to the values of the sentiments and the role of literature, partly because he was also a literary historian, alert to the frequent unnatural separation of sentiment from moral considerations by popular writers and manipulative cultural forces. Sentimentality, Thackeray insisted, should never be divorced from moral vision and the definition of human nature that makes it meaningful, and his idealizations of human nature were intended to be a thrust against the materialism and cynicism of which he was frequently accused.

Like Fielding's, Thackeray's diction often rests good-humoredly on the dividing line between worldly irony and emotional sincerity. Sometimes he is so uncomfortable with the possibility that he will be thought sentimental in the pejorative sense that he wraps his deeply felt moral sentimentality in a protective blanket of worldly irony. His sense of language is more social than psychological. Even in his sentimentalism, he is interested in creating characters from the outside, in seeing the external world clearly and sometimes ironically, rather than in creating the subjective feel of the inner life. Thackeray's sentimentality has some of the rigor of neoclassical objectivity, of a style calling attention to its common sense rather than to its tremulousness, and it is a style that rejects the compounding of emotional adjectives and sparingly utilizes the nouns of the heart. His is an accretively judgmental art in which narrative is transformed into moral evaluation, the art of the "week-day preacher" who minimizes sentimental diction because it may detract from the impact of the moral point.

Thackeray was aware that falsified sentiment frequently masquerades as sincere feeling in a meretricious combination of affectation, selfishness, and feigned nostalgia.

> They talked about the days of their youth, and Blanche was prettily sentimental. They talked about Laura, dearest Laura. . . . Blanche had loved her as a sister: was she happy with old Lady Rockminster? Wouldn't she come and stay with them at Tunbridge Wells? Oh, what walks they would take together! What songs they would sing—the old, old songs. Laura's voice was splendid. Did Arthur—she must call him Arthur—remember the songs they sang in the happy old days, now he was grown such a great man, and had such a success? Etc., etc. (*Pen*, chap. 3)

But false as it is here, Thackeray does not believe that the retrospective note is inevitably insincere. More often than not, it is Thackeray as narrator who provides the retrospective sentimental perspective.

"We must go and ask Barnes Newcome's pardon," the Colonel says, "and forgive other people's trespasses, my boy, if we hope forgiveness of our own." His voice sank down as he spoke, and he bowed his head reverently. I have heard his son tell the simple story years afterwards, with tears in his eyes. (*New*, chap. 1)

As narrator, Thackeray purposely inserts himself into and on both sides of his characters' sentimental speeches, implying that his moral mission cannot be advanced by authorial distance or aloofness, though it can be advanced by satirical displacement. In a striking descriptive passage in *Pendennis*, Thackeray provides a lesson in both false sentimentality and careful modulation of irony in the service of the idealizing moral sentiments embodied in Laura Bell.

After the scene with little Frank, in which that refractory son and heir of the house of Clavering had received the compliments in French and English, and the accompanying box on the ear from his sister, Miss Laura, who had plenty of humour, could not help calling to mind some very touching and tender verses which the Muse had read to her out of Mes Larmes [the volume of falsely sentimental poems written by Blanche], and which began, "My pretty baby brother, may angels guard thy rest," in which the Muse, after complimenting the baby upon the station in life which it was about to occupy, and contrasting it with her own lonely condition, vowed nevertheless that the angel boy would never enjoy such affection as hers was, or find in the false world before him anything so constant and tender as a sister's heart. "It may be," the forlorn one said, "it may be, you will slight it, my pretty baby sweet. You will spurn me from your bosom, I'll cling around your feet! Oh, let me, let me love you! the world will prove to you as false as 'tis to others, but I am ever true." And behold the Muse was boxing the darling brother's ears instead of kneeling at his feet, and giving Miss Laura her first lesson in the Cynical Philosophy— not quite her first, however—something like this selfishness and waywardness, something like this contrast between practice and poetry, between grand versified aspirations and everyday life, she had witnessed at home in the person of our young friend Mr. Pen. (*Pen*, chap. 1)

Laura's "first lesson in the Cynical Philosophy" does not, of course, make her a cynic. Her optimism about human nature and the moral sentiments dominates the novel.

In Thackeray's fiction, characters like Laura Bell, who have genuine moral sentiments, tend to be less expressive than those, like the "Muse," who falsely affect them. Verbal fluency usually signifies cunning rather than sincerity; the arts of speech are the arts of deceit. Becky Sharp, for example, can dazzle with verbal fluency, with the gift of turning language. She embodies the talented insincerity of the trickster who can create the conditions of sentimentality without the moral base to support it, precisely the sin for which Thackeray castigates Sterne in *The English Humourists*. To divorce the gift of language from the moral imperative is to be guilty of more than glibness. Too much talk of the "affections" (the moral sentiments) signals that the affections have been corrupted, and "she who is always speaking of her affections can have no heart" (*Pen*, chap. 1). The resolution of Dobbin's twenty-year long devotion to Amelia Sedley is expressed in a few lines of economical dialogue.

> "It was time you sent for me, dear Amelia," he said.
> "You will never go again, William."
> "No, never," he answered: and pressed the dear little soul once more to his heart. (*VF*, chap. 67)

If modern readers find the blissful moment and "the dear little soul" cloying, they miss the Victorian point—that such unions and reunions are blessed, and that the language of sentimentality embodies one of the precious realities of human nature.

Three brilliant passages from *The Newcomes* readily serve to illustrate Thackeray's delight in "sentimental scenes."[1] The first is an instance of retrospective nostalgia, untouched by the slightest breath of irony.

> In the faded ink, on the yellow paper that may have crossed and recrossed oceans, that has lain locked in chests for years, and buried under piles of family archives, while your friends have been dying and your head has grown white—who has not disinterred mementoes like these—from which the past smiles at you so sadly, shimmering out of Hades an instant but to sink back again into the cold shades, perhaps with a faint, faint sound as of a remembered tone—a ghostly echo of a once familiar laughter? I was looking, of late, at a wall in the Naples Museum, whereon a boy of Herculaneum eighteen hundred years ago had scratched with a nail the figure of a soldier. I could fancy the child turning round and smiling on after having done his etching. Which of

us that is thirty years old has not had his Pompeii? Deep
under ashes lies the Life of Youth—the careless Sport,
the Pleasure, and Passion, the darling Joy. You open an
old letterbox and look at your childish scrawls, or your
mother's letters to you when you were at school; and ex-
cavate your heart! (*New*, chap. 2)

Such retrospective sentimentality Thackeray presents as a direct route to the moral sentiments. He cannot imagine an in-
tact human being unresponsive to the feelings that the passage
describes, and the train of sentiment carries just those moral
qualities of feeling that Thackeray believes are givens of human nature.

In an earlier passage in *The Newcomes*, Thackeray plays another variation on authorial sentimentality. The voice of com-
passion and forgiveness weaves a dramatic counterpoint with
the voice of satire. The topic is the communal significance of
Colonel Newcome's disappointment in his son Clive.

The young fellow, I dare say, gave his parent no more
credit for his long self-denial than many other children
award to theirs. We take such life-offerings as our due
commonly. The old French satirist avers that, in a love-
affair, there is usually one person who loves, and the
other qui se laisse aimer; it is only in later days, perhaps,
when the treasures of love are spent, and the kind hand
cold which ministered them, that we remember how
tender it was; how soft to soothe; how eager to shield;
how ready to support and caress. The ears may no longer
hear which would have received our words of thanks so
delightedly. Let us hope those fruits of love, though
tardy, are yet not all too late; and though we bring our
tribute of reverence and gratitude, it may be to a grave-

stone, there is an acceptance even there for the stricken heart's oblation of fond remorse, contrite memories, and pious tears. I am thinking of the love of Clive Newcome's father for him (and, perhaps, young readers, of that of yours and mine for ourselves); how the old man lay awake, and devised kindnesses, and gave his all for the love of his son; and the young man took, and spent, and slept, and made merry. Did we not say, at our tale's commencement, that all stories were old? Careless prodigals and anxious elders have been from the beginning; and so may love, and repentance, and forgiveness endure even till the end. (*New*, chap. 1)

Practicing his artistry as a "week-day preacher," Thackeray offers a substitute for what scripture and the social mirror no longer provide. He defines fiction as the wisdom of distilled experience combined with the power of the moral sentiments. The authorial voice speaks to us of beginnings and endings, and it extracts from experience universal resolutions.

Though it is Clive Newcome's misfortune that he can bring his contrition and gratitude only to his father's "gravestone," Thackeray prefers to emphasize and dramatize the tributes that can be received in life. He usually protects the warm language of the moral sentiments from the cold hand of death. In a passage late in *The Newcomes*, one of the rare funeral scenes in his novels, he beautifully evokes the moral paradigms that death provides with a strength of feeling that he usually reserves for descriptions of life.

So, one day, shall the names of all of us be written there; to be deplored by how many?—to be remembered how long?—to occasion what tears, praises, sympathy, censure?—yet for a day or two, while the busy world has time to recollect us who have passed beyond it. So this poor little flower has bloomed for its little day, and pined, and withered, and perished. There was only one friend by Clive's side following the humble procession which laid poor Rosey and her child out of sight of a world that had been but unkind to her. Not many tears were there to water her lonely little grave. A grief that was akin to shame and remorse humbled him as he knelt over her. Poor little harmless lady! no more childish triumphs and vanities, no more hidden griefs are you to enjoy or suffer; and earth closes over your simple pleasures and tears! The snow was falling and whitening the coffin as they lowered it into the ground. It was at the same cemetery in which Lady Kew was buried. I dare say the same clergyman read the same service over the two graves, as he will read it for you or any of us to-morrow; and until his own turn comes. Come away from the place, poor Clive! Come sit with your orphan little boy, and bear him on your knee, and hug him to your heart. He seems yours now, and all a father's love may pour out upon him. Until this hour, Fate uncontrollable and home tyranny had separated him from you. (*New*, chap. 3)

Thackeray's art transforms potential clichés into shared experience and moral feeling, and Thackeray takes some of the sting out of death by dramatizing the theme of mutability rather than the process of dying. He prefers to reserve the language of the moral sentiments for acts of life or for philosophical generalizations. To the extent that he recognizes that Victorian commercialism exploits sentimental associations in elaborate, expensive funerals, he prefers to send those characters he thinks well of to simple graves. Unlike Dickens, he never provides death with a transcendental glow, and the disposition of the body is only of dramatic interest when its removal to the grave provides ironic comment on the moral quality of the deceased. Revolted by elaborate funerals for rotten souls, Thackeray provides Sir Pitt Crawley in *Vanity Fair* with a heartless funeral, as unsentimental as the long atrophied heart that is being buried. "The black coaches . . . ropes, palls, velvets, ostrich feathers, and other mortuary properties" bear and accompany to his grave a reprobate for whom no one mourns, except perhaps his "old pointer," who, like humankind, has a short memory. "And so Sir Pitt was forgotten—like the kindest and best of us—only a few weeks sooner." That even "the kindest and best of us" will not remain long in memory is not a statement about death or ingratitude but a gentle reminder that an awareness of universal mutability should encourage us to place our emphasis not on the anxieties of transience but on the needs of the feeling heart. Sir Pitt goes to his elaborate grave to the funereal accompaniment of moral vacuousness, the moral sentiments conspicuously absent, "the family in black coaches, with their handkerchiefs up to their noses, ready for the tears which did not come."

۔ ۔۔ویۍ 3 ﮐﯣﮯ ۔ ﻟ

What Thackeray calls "sacred tears" flow frequently in his novels. The desolate, though, always have "dry eyes." Ironically, "some of the most genuine tears that ever fall from" Becky Sharp flow when she learns, after she has wed Rawdon Crawley, that Sir Pitt is eager to marry her. Such tears, of course, are "genuine" expressions of selfish regret rather than of moral feeling. For the wasteland of the atrophied heart has no revivifying waters, and an insufficiency of moral sentiment produces emotional aridity.

Thackeray can be playfully ironic about the sacredness of tears, provided that the irony reinforces rather than denies their sacredness. When her brother hints at the possibility that she may remarry, Amelia Sedley has, "as usual, recourse to the water-works" (*VF*, chap. 59). Her eyes blur with a sincerity of moral feeling that makes Thackeray's gentle irony an affirmation of the value of her tears. To repress tears is unnatural, to misuse them is perverse. Thackeray connects the calculated misuse of tears to the misuse of sentimentality for self-serving ends, the separation, as in Sterne, of the techniques of sentimentality from the moral sentiments. When Amelia parts from her son, "the tender heart overflowed, and taking the boy to her breast, she . . . wept silently over him in a sainted agony of tears" (*VF*, chap. 50). Becky willingly parts from her son, without shedding a tear for anyone. Blanche Amory proudly authors a book of poems called *Mes Larmes*, cultivating her sentiments for public display. But "this young lady," Thackeray tells us, "was not able to carry out any emotion to the full; but had a sham enthusiasm, a sham hatred, a sham love, a sham taste, a sham grief, each of which flared and shone very vehemently for an instant, but subsided and gave place to the next sham emotion" (*Pen*, chap. 3).

Conscious of the frequency of the "water-works" and the potential for misunderstanding, Thackeray was alert to the possibility that he himself might be accused of insincerely manipulating his reader's feelings.[2] Like other Victorian sentimental writers, however, he believed that the artist instinctively makes craftsmanship an expression of moral feeling. The devices of sentiment develop naturally from the core of feeling that is the source of art. Sentimental writers like Thackeray strongly identify with the moral worth of their characters and establish a bond of sincerity between themselves and their readers, creating a community of three classes—characters, readers, and authors—the latter two of which acknowledge that they share a definition of human nature. Genuine tears are not a literary manipulation, and, though all sorrows in fiction are "paper sorrows," art does not mediate between artifice and reality, between sentimental devices and the moral sentiments. True art reveals their inseparability. The mirror held up to Human Nature is either true to Human Nature or not.

Aware that the author's claim to sincerity is subject to the same skepticism as his characters' tears, that they are, in fact, the same issue, Thackeray exerts himself to find some convincing way to affirm the sincerity of Amelia's tears and to disarm dry-eyed skepticism. Unlike Dickens, he finds the direct assault unattractive. He does not, usually, attempt to overcome resistance with a full-scale, unmediated, single-toned barrage of emotional ammunition. His model is Fielding, not Richardson. With the resources of a formal education and an urbane temperament, he makes his appeal for credibility with humor, pathos, gentle irony, a mixture of the comic and the serious, and with literary allusions. When Dobbin proclaims that Amelia and he will never part again, Little George "flung his arms around his mother. As for that lady: let us say what she did in the words of a favourite poet—Askpruoev Yellassa (smiling through her tears)." As in Fielding's description of Sophia, the mock-heroic allusion to the *Iliad* elevates rather than deflates. Though we may smile at and, from our superior worldly position, sometimes even condescend to Amelia, we are never to doubt that she or Thackeray are any the less sincere in their sentiments because of her "water-works" or his indirect, slightly ironic presentation.

Thackeray does share the Victorian belief that women cry more readily than men for reasons that have to do with the special aspects of human nature that are feminine rather than with cultural conditioning. Women by nature have their moral sentiments closer to the surface of expression than men and have not been as subject to the eroding contaminations of institutional education and the marketplace. Since women, then, lend themselves more easily than men to idealization in fiction, Thackeray not only finds it easier to locate their moral sentiments but also associates "the floodgates" with gender rather than with the individual.

> How the floodgates were opened and mother and daughter wept, when they were together embracing each other in this sanctuary, may readily be imagined by every reader who possesses the least sentimental turn. When don't ladies weep? At what occasion of joy, sorrow, or other business of life? and, after such an event as a marriage mother and daughter were surely at liberty to give way to a sensibility which is as tender as it is refreshing. About a question of marriage I have seen women who hate each other kiss and cry together quite fondly. How much more do they feel when they love! Good mothers are married over again at their daughters' weddings: and as for subsequent events, who does not know how ultra-maternal grandmothers are?—in fact a woman, until she is a grandmother, does not often really know what to be a mother is. Let us respect Amelia and her mama whispering and whimpering and laughing and crying in the parlour and the twilight. (*VF*, chap. 26)

Though "genuine tears" are redemptive and women have more ready access to them than men, not all women, of course, remain true to their innate moral sentiments. If there are women whose moral sentiments cannot be diminished, there are also those who cannot withstand the pressure of a corrupt or deprived environment. The world frequently barters with feeling, and tears are calculatingly regulated by the social marketplace. Becky, for example, cannot cry, her natural sentiments unnaturally repressed. "Miss Bullock knows how to regulate her feelings better than [Amelia]. . . . Miss B. would never have committed herself as that imprudent Amelia had done; pledged her love irretrievably; confessed her heart away, and got nothing back." The narrative provides the ironic distancing and the affirmation of the sentiments: "Be cautious then, young ladies; be wary how you engage. Be shy of loving frankly; never tell all you feel, or (a better way still) feel very little" (*VF*, chap. 18). For if one practices repression of the feelings, one will soon have very little left to practice on.

Men resort to the "water-works" so infrequently that their tears cannot be the subject of even gentle irony. Thackeray's male characters cry only in the most desperate or passionate circumstances. In Rawdon Crawley, Thackeray provides his most effective dramatization of genuine tears as the visible expression of the moral sentiments. Rawdon's male credentials are impeccable: soldier, adventurer, gambler, lover, a talented, much-admired expert at all the minor masculine arts of survival practiced by the wellborn. His social milieu has successfully repressed his moral feeling. Surviving on "nothing a year," Rawdon's predatory habits adhere to the code of the society and the family that have created him. He is a victim of the society that approves his victimization of others.

Thackeray is marvelously adroit in creating in Rawdon a

character whose reserves of moral sentiment have been obscured but not obliterated by gentlemanly sloth and social corruption. Though it operates within the limits of his social code, Rawdon's sincerity is never in question. By maintaining Rawdon's basic likability, Thackeray reserves the possibility, without being explicit, that the time will come when Rawdon will redeem himself. At his worst, Rawdon never acts in a way that excludes the possibility of our feeling moral affection for him. The time does come. Rawdon is imprisoned for debt and expects Becky to obtain his release. When Jane Southwood comes instead, Rawdon, aware now that his wife does not respect let alone love him, "was quite overcome by that kind voice and presence. He ran up to her—caught her in his arms—gasped out some inarticulate words of thanks, and fairly sobbed on her shoulder." Rawdon's tears reflect the awakening of his innate moral sentiments. He

> thanked his sister a hundred times, and with an ardour of gratitude which touched and almost alarmed that soft-hearted woman. "Oh," said he, in his rude, artless way, "you—you don't know how I'm changed since I've known you—and Little Rawdy. I—I'd like to change somehow. You see I want—I want—to be—." He did not finish the sentence, but she could interpret it. (*VF*, chap. 53)

What he wants to be is "good." In fact, at that moment he already *is* good. Having discovered his moral sentiments, he has become a moral man and possesses a means of expressing them that transcends words. Determined to duel with Lord Steyne, Rawdon discusses his son with Captain Macmurdo.

> "He's a regular trump, that boy. . . . I say, Mac, if any-

thing goes wrong—if I drop—I should like you to—to go and see him, you know: and say that I was very fond of him, and that. And—dash it—old chap, give him these gold sleeve-buttons: it's all I've got." He covered his face with his black hands; over which the tears rolled and made furrows of white. Mr. Macmurdo had also occasion to take off his silk night-cap and rub it across his eyes. (*VF*, chap. 54)

⚜ 4 ⚜

Many dramatic incidents in Thackeray's novels turn on the question of whether the heart will have and act on moral sentiments. The commitment to the moral sentiments demands an optimistic social paradigm, and Thackeray, like Dickens, invests so heavily in the innateness of the moral sentiments that he can do nothing other than provide happy endings for his novels. He may qualify the happiness with gentle irony, as in the union of Amelia and William in *Vanity Fair*, but the irony reinforces rather than undermines the victory of the moral sentiments. Not surprisingly, the social paradigm that Thackeray most frequently uses to represent the victory of the moral sentiments is the joining of lovers in marriage. Society provides the ritual affirmation of its belief that the moral sentiments may be enriched in a special union which symbolizes that all division and discord can be made whole and harmonious. For the Victorians in general, an art that embodied such harmonies was not a compromise with popular taste or commercial demand but an affirmation of the inseparability of aesthetic and moral vision.

Thackeray conceives of plot partly as a system for allocating rewards and punishments in a serial development that concludes with an affirmation of the moral sentiments. Undeserving characters usually receive banal punishments, and for Becky and Lord Steyne the appropriate punishment is the absence of rewards. They are deprived of the blessings of the moral sentiments. But Laura and Pendennis, Ethel and Clive, and Amelia and Dobbin marry, the highest reward, and Henry Esmond is united with "the truest and tenderest and purest wife ever man was blessed with" (*HE*, chap. 3). That Thackeray makes it clear that Dobbin's marriage will have its exasperating moments does not detract from the marriage as an ideal model and from Amelia as a representation of the ideal moral sentiments. Thackeray never loses sight of the realities of daily life and of the minor crosses one may have to bear as the price of great virtues. Though Amelia may sometimes be a burden to Dobbin, the qualities that make some modern readers ambivalent about her are those that Dobbin and the Victorians regard as the highest of human nature. Some modern readers may find Amelia vapid, weepy, even wearisome. Thackeray recognizes this aspect of Amelia. But he values goodness more than interestingness: goodness comes before dullness. And Dobbin clearly would rather have a good dull wife than a bad exciting one. From the Victorian point of view, no man can have a wife who is both good and exciting.

Unlike some modern readers, Thackeray thinks this no loss at all. The focus of human interest should be, he believes, moral attractiveness. Mrs. Pendennis is one of these idealized women who have "natural sweetness and kindness," and "in whose angelical natures there is something awful as well as beautiful, to contemplate . . . that adorable purity which never seems to do or to think wrong" (*Pen*, chap. 1). She is fully defined in terms of her moral sentiments. That she must maintain her "purity" within the confines of domestic life seems quite acceptable to Thackeray. Women, like Becky, who roll up their sleeves to work in the world, usually dirty their hands. In Becky's case, the erosion of innate moral sentiments and a pattern of self-calculating aggression have made her into an appropriate companion for Lord Steyne rather than for Rawdon Crawley. But there are instances of "angelical natures" that are human natures, and the more we allow our innate moral sentiments to flourish, the closer we come to being compared justifiably to angelic natures idealized beyond their humanness. The comparison comes easily to Victorian sentimentalists.

> For Dobbin was very soft-hearted. The sight of women and children in pain always used to melt him. The idea of Amelia broken-hearted and lonely, tore that good-natured soul with anguish. And he broke out into an emotion, which anybody who likes may consider unmanly. He swore that Amelia was an angel. . . . And for himself, he blushed with remorse and shame, as the remembrance of his own selfishness and indifference contrasted with that perfect purity. (*VF*, chap. 18)

The hagiography needs to be taken seriously as a Victorian cultural image, though Thackeray makes clear throughout *Vanity Fair* that Amelia is also a fallible creature whose faults are of the sort that do not detract from but actually strengthen her role as an idealization of the moral sentiments. The more Thackeray sees men as deficient in moral sentiment and repressed in their ability to express whatever sentiment they do have, the more use he has for female idealizations. The same gender-based iconography supports Pendennis' sense of the moral splendor of both his mother's and Laura Bell's natures.

> Ah, sister, how weak and wicked we [men] are; how spotless and full of love and truth, Heaven made you! I think for some of you there has been no fall. . . . You can't help having sweet thoughts, and doing good actions. Dear creature! they are the flower which you bear. (*Pen*, chap. 3)

Though aware that some women might refuse to bear such flowers, or even might prefer "fleurs de mal," Thackeray did not imagine that his readers might think them too heavy or too sweet. He appreciated the possibility that some might find such idealizations aesthetically uninteresting, "namby-pamby milk-and-water affected" creatures (*VF*, chap. 42). But Thackeray, who was not of Becky's "party without knowing it," most respected moral energy, for the expenditure of energy itself is an authentication of neither being nor worth, except to the extent that it serves a moral purpose.[3] What do we admire more, he asked, and what do we get more pleasure from, intellect or goodness? The evidence of experience, Thackeray believed, supports the conclusion that intellect is rarely in the service of the moral sentiments, and that we derive the highest pleasure from and have the most admiration for moral performance. Inevitably, then, Thackeray would rather we be good—and true to our innate natures—than be interesting. If we are good, however, and value goodness, then we will take pleasure in such feelings, as Adam Smith claims our natures demand, and change our definition of what is interesting.

Thackeray's sophistication in playing with the various levels of truth in fiction and subordinating literal reality to moral

models is nowhere more effectively realized than at the conclusion of *The Newcomes* (chap. 3). The narrator, who claims
that he has heard Clive Newcome's story from Pendennis,
asks, with some disappointment, "might he not have told us
whether Miss Ethel married anybody finally? It was provoking
that he should retire to the shades without answering that sentimental question." The narrator, though, does have some
vague impressions on the matter, which he grants may or may
not be accurate, and he thinks it likely that Clive and Ethel
married. "But have they any children?" the narrator asks. And
the voice of Thackeray as narrator puts an end to the inquiry
by reminding us that all such questions deal with hopes, with
"paper sorrows," in a genre that, for Thackeray, is about providing models rather than simple mirrors.

> But for you, dear friend, it is as you like. You may settle
> your fable-land in your own fashion. . . . And the poet of
> fable-land rewards and punishes absolutely. He splen-
> didly deals out bags of sovereigns, which won't buy any-
> thing; belabors wicked backs with awful blows, which do
> not hurt: endows heroines with preternatural beauty,
> and creates heroes, who, if ugly sometimes, yet possess a
> thousand good qualities, and usually end by being im-
> mensely rich; makes the hero and heroine happy at last,
> and happy ever after. Ah, happy harmless fable-land,
> where these things are! Friendly reader! may you and the
> author meet there on some future day! He hopes so; as he
> yet keeps a lingering hold of your hand, and bids you
> farewell with a kind heart.

Thackeray dramatizes simultaneously the text and the text-
creator, the fable and the reality out of which the fable arises.
In the conflation, the reader both participates in and creates

personal variations on the fable whose ultimate text is the "fable-land" of literature. One of Thackeray's earliest appreciators remarked that "he could not have painted *Vanity Fair* as he has, unless Eden had been shining brightly in his eyes."[4] Thackeray's Eden has no transcendental location; it is the imagined "fable-land," the fiction that provides models of human nature and the moral sentiments.

⌁————ⵗ 5 ⵗ————⌁

Defining goodness as a function of social approval, Becky Sharp claims that she would have been "a good woman" if only she had "had 5000 a year."

> "I could pay everybody if I had but the money. This is what the conjurors here pride themselves upon doing. They look down with pity upon us miserable sinners who have none. They think themselves generous if they give our children a five pound note, and us contemptible if we are without one." And who knows but Rebecca was right in her speculations—and that it was only a question of money and fortune which made the difference between her and an honest woman? If you take temptations into account, who is to say that he is better than his neighbor? . . . An alderman coming from a turtle feast will not step out of his carriage to steal a leg of mutton; but put him to starve, and see if he will not purloin the load. Becky consoled herself by so balancing the changes and equalizing the distribution of good and evil in the world. (*VF*, chap. 41)

But that it is not *only* a question of money Thackeray states

clearly throughout *Vanity Fair*. When poor, Amelia retains
her goodness. When relatively prosperous, Becky acts badly.
Her behavior is not criminal, however, but immoral, and
Thackeray provides the contrast between the well-fed and the
starving alderman as an ironic dramatization of the putative
extremes of "good" and "evil" rather than as an example rel-
evant to Becky's situation. Thackeray, in fact, hardly believes
in good and evil at all, but in good and less good, and eventually so little good that we seem to have lost sight of good entirely. Though he hopes for a world in which theft will not be
necessary, he does not have a serious argument with those who
steal in order to feed themselves. Criminal liability is irrelevant to moral feeling, and Becky, who always remains within
the law, is condemned for acting against a higher law, natural
law.

What is "human nature?" What is "natural" human behavior and what is "unnatural" human behavior? Thackeray constantly asks in providing moral glosses for his characters.
Though, like many of his contemporaries, he occasionally
gives "nature," "natural," and "unnatural" some local meaning, generally he uses the terms to mean that human beings
have innate dispositions. "Nature" in this sense usually has an
adjectival qualification. "Dobbin," for example, "was of too
simple and generous a nature," "Mr. Jos . . . was by no means
an ill-natured person," and Amelia has a "sweet and affection-
ate nature" (*VF*, chaps. 60, 58, 31). Thackeray posits an underlying constant, human nature, from which all actions and
states derive. His characters act out of their natures rather
than have their natures formed or modified by their actions.
Thus "it was this young woman's [Amelia's] nature . . . to sac-
rifice herself and to fling all that she had at the feet of the beloved object," whereas Becky "was of a wild, roving nature,

inherited from father and mother, who were both Bohemians, by taste and circumstance" (*VF*, chaps. 57, 65). Dobbin provides the definitive Thackerayan comment, the distillation of authorial wisdom, on the matter.

> In reply to some faint objection of Mrs. Amelia's (taken from certain theological works like the "Washerwoman of Finchley Common" and others of that school, with which Mrs. Osborne had been furnished during her life at Brompton) he told her an eastern fable of the owl who thought that the sunshine was unbearable for the eyes, and that the Nightingale was a most over-rated bird. "It is one's nature to sing and the other to hoot," he said, laughing, "and with such a sweet voice as you have yourself, you must belong to the Bulbul [nightingale] faction." (*VF*, chap. 62)

Though Thackeray shares Dickens' belief in the moral sentiments, he allows to a greater degree that even someone who has strong moral sentiments can make a serious mistake in which the heart bestows itself upon an unworthy object. Amelia does belong to the "Bulbul faction." The nightingale, though, sings in an ordinary garden and sometimes misinterprets the local cacophony. Those for whom there has been "no fall" may make the occasional errors of the innocent, for their innate moral sentiments cannot always protect them from misjudgment. Even more than Dickens', Thackeray's characters are born into the hard shells of their natures, which give them very little room for growth and little potential for shedding their old natures and growing new ones. Rather than grow better selves, they at best divest themselves of what the world has done to them, like taking off a layer of clothes that belongs to someone else. When Dickens' characters need to divest themselves of environmental clothes, there always turn out to be many layers, one of which may be a straitjacket. And when they strip, they find either that they have a more complicated, mysterious nakedness or human nature to work with or, simply, that stripping completely is impossible. The environmental clothes cling to the body and there are more of them.

The characters in Thackeray's fiction, then, seem to have been born into their natures, some to sing, others to hoot. Environment can influence action. But, though "remorse is the least active of all a man's moral sense—the very easiest to be deadened when wakened," in some it is "never wakened at all" (*VF*, chap. 42). The inevitable question, why do some people have more and some less of the moral sentiments, and who or what is responsible for both the amounts and the distribution, Thackeray responds to by saying, in effect, that answering such questions is not the function of the novelist or at least that his self-definition as a novelist does not require that he provide answers. Insofar as an answer might be physiological, he claims incompetence; insofar as an answer might be theological, he claims that it is outside his province. Thackeray assumes that such complications are beyond human unraveling, and though the complications may rise to mysteries, as they do for Dickens, Thackeray prefers to see the situation in the most pragmatic, local terms possible. Since there is no way of determining responsibility for the schema, including the unequal number and the odd distribution of nightingales and owls, he finds it pointless to be too hard on the owls and unwise not to admire the nightingales. At the same time, he posits an available moral yardstick, the distinction between "natural" and "unnatural" performance. The former is the spontaneous expression of the innate moral sentiments. Those who do not honor nature's most life-giving and life-preserving feelings and relationships are "unnatural."

Becky's inability to "like" her son is the most telling comment Thackeray can make on her "unnaturalness." And Lady Jane, remonstrating with Sir Pitt, who has defended Becky, emphasizes that Becky's wickedness resides in her being "a heartless mother, a false wife." For "she never loved her dear little boy, who used to fly here and tell me of her cruelty to him" (*VF*, chap. 55). When, to Becky's technically correct claim that she "is innocent," Rawdon responds that she is in fact "as bad as guilty," Thackeray intends to raise the discourse to the ultimate distinction between "natural" and "unnatural," which no technicalities can possibly address. Becky has rejected the highest obligation of human nature, which is to accept its nature, to allow the natural moral sentiments to flourish.

It is best, of course, to belong to, to be born into, the "Bulbul faction." But the world has many owls, and Thackeray finds a necessary place for them. Becky, who is one of the owls, helps to provide, in the interactions between the owls and the nightingales, the tension and the dialectic that allow the novelist to create the "fable-land" of idealization. Thackeray denies that the nightingale's song is overrated. On the contrary, the idealization can never be over-appreciated or too highly valued. Though the mixed nature of most human beings provides the background for the counterpoint between the owls and the nightingales, Thackeray never wants the realistic background to overshadow the idealistic foreground. Becky sings the coarse songs of this world; Amelia sings to "the spirit ditties of no tone." Thackeray is aware of the difficulty his contemporaries have in hearing Amelia's melody, to which modern readers are generally even more tone-deaf than Victorian readers. But he expects that the response to both Becky and Amelia will be through the instinctive moral sentiments, and there Amelia has the advantage.

The Reign of Sentimentality

After attending Thackeray's lectures on *The English Humour-ists*, Thomas Carlyle remarked that "there is a great deal of talent in him, a great deal of sensibility,—irritability, sensuality, vanity without limit;—and nothing, or little, but sentimentalism and play-actorism to guide it all with."[1] Carlyle was the most articulate, widely read Victorian opponent of sentimentality, though there are deep currents within his work that run counter to or at least give a tug of ambivalence to his anti-sentimentality. Carlyle responded positively to some aspects of eighteenth-century sentimental literature to a greater extent than his principles would seem to sanction, and two elements within his writing have a sentimental base, his emphasis on his own feelings as innately moral and his idealization of the hero and the heroic. His voice, though, was more heard than listened to. Carlyle's sentimentality, in the long run, confirmed rather than disputed the widespread view that human nature was being devalued, a devaluation to which, he believed, sentimentality was contributing. Unlike Dickens and Thackeray, he expressed the ambivalence and inconsistency of those Victorians who anticipated twentieth-century hostility to sentimentality without being immune to the feelings to which sentimentality appeals or liberated from the needs which it fulfills.

Feeling itself is a troublesome element for Carlyle, mainly

because it seemed to him that many of his contemporaries celebrated the value of feeling independent of moral action. Unlike most Victorians, he used the word *sensibility* rather than *sentiment* to refer to the vehicle of moral feeling. Sensibility, for Carlyle, is the capacity to respond to truth. Sentimentality is the application of sensibility to falsehood, to untruth. Sensibility, then, is the origin of all feeling, and sincere feeling that remains as close as possible to its fountainhead in the unconscious is a moral force. In Carlyle's view, Thackeray's sentimentality, and sentimentality in general, is sensibility warped by illusions, commingled with falsehoods, and without moral purpose or control.

Carlyle struggled persistently to close the gap between feeling and action. Both his Romantic and his religious background suggested to him that "sincerity" was the moral dimension of personality that provided the qualitative mechanism needed to unite feeling and action. Like Matthew Arnold, he was alert to the danger of feeling turned in upon itself, liberated from the responsibility to act that moral vision imposes. Without an effective controlling mechanism, sensibility threatened to become solipsism, a world of "I-eyty," of the ego run wild. To combat such a threat, which had risen already to the level of a widespread condition in modern culture, Carlyle emphasized the importance of some controlling "other," outside the self, either as physical reality, to be seen with one's eyes, or as historical vision, to be reconstructed by the imagination, or as cosmic vision, to be perceived by the inner eye. For whatever is perceived through sensibility must be transformed into a moral structure—a substantive statement—by the power of sincerity and the clarity of moral vision.

Carlyle advocates the kind of "thrift" or economy in feeling that self-reflexive sensibilities rarely promote in order to distinguish further between his definition of sensibility and the widespread late eighteenth-century and Romantic notion of sensibility as the disposition to feel without moral or structural restraint. Whereas intellectual thriftlessness is a waste of logical motion, uneconomical emotional expenditure is a waste of spirit. "How much wasterfuller still," Carlyle comments, "is it to *feel about Feeling*" (*CME*, vol. 4, p. 109). "Subjective" literature, Carlyle believes, embodies a self-consciousness about feeling that places expression of feeling at least one remove from the feelings themselves. This displacement produces the damaging self-consciousness of Romanticism as well as the moral falsity of sentimentality.

Since as a writer Carlyle himself participates in the self-consciousness about feeling that he condemns, his analysis is partly self-criticism. While he grants that it is the fate of all modern writers and writing to suffer from the disease of self-consciousness, he acknowledges that his own commitment to autobiography as the point of departure for literature increases the waste of spirit. In fact, that waste of spirit becomes part of his subject matter, and the central concern of Carlyle's writing is the paradox of his own self-consciousness. From *Sartor Resartus* to *Frederick the Great*, he reveals himself struggling unsuccessfully to avoid being the kind of subjective writer he deplores. In writing about Rahel von Ense, whom he admired, he creates a critique that the modern reader, following Carlyle's lead, might turn back upon him. Rahel's letters

> do not suit us at all. They are subjective letters . . . not objective; the grand material of them is endless depictur-

ing of moods, sensations, miseries, joys and lyrical conditions of the writer; no definite picture drawn, or rarely any, of persons, transactions or events. . . . To what end, to what end? we always ask. Not by looking at itself, but by looking at things out of itself, and ascertaining and ruling these, shall the mind become known. (*CME*, vol. 4, p. 108)

Carlyle's own capacity to create "pictures" of people and events served him well, and his criticism of Rahel functioned partly as self-warning and self-guidance.

Carlyle believed that a science of mind is impossible, partly because the self is contained within the mind and not the mind within the self, partly because his definition of mind is so all-inclusive that a comprehension of mind in its totality is beyond our capability. But we can know a portion of our minds, that portion that is synonymous with the self. And we know that portion of the mind that is the self through those innate responses of the self to the self and to the external world. Such innate responses are basic to our human nature. They are intuitive, spontaneous, and the function of feeling or sensibility rather than thought. Such unmediated, spontaneous knowing of the self through sensibility should lead to action, to the narrowing, even the elimination, of the potential gap between feeling and action. Sensibility has its dangers, of course, as in Rahel's case: an overly keen sensibility may separate itself from the moral imperative that directs feeling toward social concerns and cosmic truths. Such self-reflexive and uncontrolled sensibilities are readily debased into sentimentality, prone to mistake keenness of feeling for moral essence and to trust not in some higher good but in the goodness of human nature.

Carlyle, who read widely in eighteenth-century literature and philosophy, suffered through much of his youth the burden of recognizing the brilliance of many eighteenth-century arguments against Christianity. He derived the strength to reject the dominant eighteenth-century view of human nature partly from its very integrity and cogency and partly from his energizing awareness of what power he would need to overcome such formidable opponents. But his rejection was not primarily of the particulars of moral conduct but of the tone and the view of human potential that moral philosophy promoted. Like the moral philosophers, Carlyle believed that the feelings are the source of values and conduct. He struggled through to the position, consistent with Dickens and Thackeray, that social conditioning counted less in mankind's affairs than did innate qualities of human nature. But he defined human nature, emphatically in opposition to Hume and Smith, as a battleground where good and evil struggle vigorously for a victory which good has the likelier chance to achieve. Human nature is not innately good. It is variegated, complicated, mysterious, beyond categories and formulas. Sensibility, the capacity for sincere response through and of the feelings, one among a number of basic elements in human nature, needed to be encouraged to flourish, and then, flourishing, it needed mechanisms of control in life and in literature. Sentimentality seemed to Carlyle reductive, intent on defining man only in human terms, reducing human nature to one of its aspects, making formulas out of mysteries and driving God out of man.

Carlyle struggled against sentimentality, partly because he recognized the overlap between sensibility and sentimentality and the dangerous tendency of sensibility to reject moral control; partly because eighteenth-century moral philosophers, especially Hume, seemed brilliant, even incontrovertible, on the rational level; partly because the dominant tone of pre- and early Victorian Whig culture, in opposition to which he came to intellectual manhood, was eighteenth-century rationalism; and partly because as a young man he had responded warmly to eighteenth-century writers, particularly the novelists, who were strong advocates of sentimental values. The aesthetic and intellectual pleasure he derived from Enlightenment literature extended to Enlightenment ideas. Though he read German and Italian writers, he read most widely in the French writers of the period, a crucial experience in the development of his mild Francophobia. The most odious form of nineteenth-century sentimentality he regarded as an infection that had originated in France and had spread to Britain in the guise of the French novel and "Phallus-worship."[2]

To the extent that sentimentality was an Enlightenment phenomenon, it seemed to Carlyle hopelessly devitalized by mechanism, particularly by deism and natural religion. The limitations of eighteenth-century culture had prevented its potential heroes, from Frederick the Great to Napoleon, from becoming the Cromwells they might have been. Mechanism had devitalized Voltaire, Diderot, and Hume, and even Samuel Johnson's titanic powers could not fully overcome the dominant tendencies of the age. Like William Blake, Carlyle had no use for subtleties and qualifications in his broad condemnation of the culture whose values he detested. He judged all eighteenth-century European culture to be corrosively tarnished with the language and values of mechanism, whose ultimate strength was like sand thrown into the power of the divine storm through whose force "Israel's tents do shine so bright."[3] Since sentimentality attempted to define human nature in a language and according to principles derived from Enlightenment assumptions, Carlyle, with a broad brush, painted sentimentality and mechanism the same unattractive color.

His broad brush also condemned Benevolence. Carlyle believed that eighteenth-century moral philosophy had contaminated Victorian culture with a mistaken notion of social responsibility, part of the Enlightenment's "windy sentimentality" (*HHW*, chap. 5, p. 176). Though Carlyle thought Benevolence a secularization, and consequently a corruption, of charity, he also considered even traditional Pauline charity a rationalization for evading social responsibility. In a community in which there was widespread unemployment, poverty, and disease, Christian charity, in Carlyle's view, provided an unsound, ineffective substitute for the government-sponsored and -administered social programs he believed were necessary to deal with national and international misery. Personal and private charity could not deal with, and in fact become an excuse to avoid dealing with, "the Irish Giant" called "Despair."

Carlyle's detestation of Benevolence was motivated mainly, though, by his belief that "universal" projects for "the good of the species" suffer the inherent futility of failing to focus on the important field of action, the individual. Benevolence, he told Mill, is the doctrine of

> Socinian Preachers [who believe that the universe is rational and material]. . . . I cannot so much as imagine any peace or solid foundation of improvement in human things till this universal scheme of procedure go out of men's heads again, and each take to what alone is prac-

ticable for himself—mending of his own ways;—where-
from Benevolence enough, and infinitely better things,
will be sure enough to result.[4]

The philanthropic tendency to devote resources to improving
other people and countries, satirized by Dickens in his portrait of Mrs. Jellyby in *Bleak House*, usually encourages eva-
sion of the primary responsibility to improve oneself. But
Dickens' criticism of benevolence ends where Carlyle's be-
gins, for, like Thackeray, Dickens does not connect sentimentality to moral irresponsibility and laissez-faire capitalism.
Within eighteenth- and early nineteenth-century fiction, sentiment is presented with little regard to actual social conditions, and Dickens' benevolent avatars, like Mr. Pickwick and
Mr. Brownlow, are admirable citizens whose private charities
define the limits of their social consciousness. Whereas Carlyle finds the eighteenth-century influence a cultural burden,
Dickens envisions it at worst as a benign, conservative anach-
ronism, only dangerous if we try to travel on a stagecoach in
an age of steam.

How strongly eighteenth-century views influenced the Victorians is revealed in how fully Thackeray embraces and Carlyle rejects them, the former a representative of Victorian
middle-of-the-road Anglican conservatism, the latter a representative of Victorian radical Puritan conservatism. Thackeray
popularized the previous century's literature at a time when
more narrow standards of propriety made the "humourists"
less widely read. His supreme puppet show, *Vanity Fair*, advocated the value of sentimentality based on the doctrine of
the moral sentiments. Carlyle, associating the moral sentiments and sentimentality with eighteenth-century mechanism, which lacked seriousness and was spiritually blind,

found his Puritan imagination haunted by these destructive ghosts. Against the grain of personal fondness, he questioned Thackeray's moral sincerity and found his sentimentality either cynical or recklessly uncontrolled.

Carlyle also associated sentimentality with what he believed to be two dangerous aspects of Romanticism, popular Byronism and Romantic and post-Romantic sensuality. Actually, Carlyle's own "Byronism," particularly within *Sartor Resartus* though actually lifelong, provides a counterbalance to his notorious request that his readers close their copies of Byron and open their copies of Goethe.[5] To Carlyle, Byron represented the willful modern iconoclast elevating the Self into both the worshipper and the worshipped, while Goethe represented the modern spiritual pilgrim searching for fundamental truths that transcend the limitations of the Self. Carlyle spent much of his early career struggling with these competing influences. Though Byron left his mark, Carlyle rejected the Byronic mode of the Self liberated from traditional moral and social control. Popular Byronism, in Carlyle's judgment, perverted sensibility into ego-sensibility, elevating the Self into a god and divorcing feeling from moral control and moral action. Carlyle, like numbers of Thackeray's contemporaries, took strong "objection . . . to the manner in which" Thackeray "exalted sentiment above duty" and feared that sentimentality in general was infected by such a disposition.[6]

Sentimentality also seemed to Carlyle a primary lubricant of Romantic sensuality, greasing the wheels that travel to George Sandism and Phallus-worship. Much of his hostility to sentimentality derived from his conviction that a doctrine of the primacy of the feelings is inseparable from a doctrine of the primacy of sex. Aware of the erotic potential of language, Carlyle decried the widespread modern effort to liberate language from its traditional moral mission. Conveniently, the main eighteenth-century propagators of the sexual revolution were French, not English, and among the philosophical sentimentalists, Rousseau was primarily responsible for legitimizing literary eroticism.

> His Books, like himself, are what I call unhealthy. . . . [His] sensuality . . . combined with such an intellectual gift . . . makes pictures of a certain gorgeous attractiveness: but they are not genuinely poetical. Not white sunlight: something operatic; a kind of rosepink, artificial bedizenment. It is frequent, or rather it is universal, among the French since his time. Madame de Stael has something of it; St. Pierre, and down onwards to the present astonishing convulsionary "Literature of Desperation." (*HHW*, chap. 5, p. 187)

England was being exposed to a plague of French literary sensuality. Though a thousand and one minor French novelists and English imitators flourished, two of whom, George Henry Lewes and Geraldine Jewsbury, were friends of the Carlyles, the most prominent perpetrator of this venereal disease was George Sand, the chief goddess of the new Phallus-worship. Literary sentimentality was both vehicle and shrine of the "New Sand Religion."[7]

By modern standards, Lewes's *Ranthorpe* (1845) and Jewsbury's *Zoe, The History of Two Lives* (1845), to take two representative examples that Carlyle read, hardly descend to the level of even soft-core pornography.[8] Nevertheless, the "rosepink" sensuality of the language describing the feelings and the activities of the novels' main characters seemed to Carlyle unacceptably erotic, exemplifying the spread of the George Sand disease from France to England. In Carlyle's view, the rise of democracy, the decline of religious standards and authority, the elimination of the sacred from daily life, and the transformation of provincial nations into an international European community rendered British Victorian culture especially susceptible to French literary eroticism. By nature and natural right, Carlyle believed, Britain and the other northern European countries were a bastion of moral integrity, "white sunlight" rather than "rosepink," a providential nation. "Look at a Shakespeare, at a Goethe, even at a Walter Scott," he urged, comparing them to Rousseau and George Sand. Protestant north European culture traditionally could distinguish "the True from the Sham-True," the spiritual from the sensual (*HHW*, chap. 5, p. 187). But such moral vision was on the decline, even in Britain, increasingly blinded as it was by the "rosepink" eroticism spread by the sentimental novel.

Carlyle granted that Dickens and Thackeray had avoided George Sandism in its most virulent form. Though he recognized the difference, however, he could not separate the doctrine of the sentiments as moral from fictional representations of the sentiments as pleasurable. Within the sentimental tradition, as modified by literary realism, the novel, even the novel he most deeply admired, Goethe's *Wilhelm Meister*, suffered the necessity of dramatizing the tactile experiences of daily life. The very nature of fiction promoted the dangers of sensuality, especially novels that emphasized the sentiments associated with loving and being in love, with romantic attachments.

> Altogether false and damnable that love should be represented as spreading itself over our whole existence, and constituting one of the grand interests of it; whereas love—the thing people call love—is confined to a very

131

few years of man's life; to, in fact a quite insignificant fraction of it, and even then is but one thing to be attended to among many infinitely more important things.[9]

Carlyle also opposed "the reign of Sentimentality" because he thought its self-consciousness about "virtue" and "doing good" was self-evidently "unhealthy," an instance of the disease of self-consciousness in the modern world. In his influential essay "Characteristics" (1831), he grants that unselfconsciousness, the spontaneous expression of one's innate spiritual feelings, is an ideal, unrealizable state. Yet that is "ever the goal towards which our actual state of being strives; which it is the more perfect the nearer it can approach" (*CME*, vol. 3, p. 8). Like the moral philosophers, Carlyle believed that people have innate "generous affections." But he also believed that they are part of a larger energy field with diverse elements, some of which demand mechanisms of control, and part of a struggle in which the Hobbesian view of man as a creature who sometimes must be controlled by authority for the good of the commonwealth has its place. For Carlyle, human nature is a dynamic entity, a constant part of process, transcending reason and mechanism. The ultimate authority is the self-authenticating divine nature within human beings which provides the moral ideals that people strive to fulfill. In the striving, Carlyle suggests, is our moral essence.

Like Dickens, Carlyle considers the possibility that personal and social corruption have been historically determined (both writers define historical determinism as the influence of the past on the present rather than as inevitable patterns within historical process). Neither, though, accepts the claim that people are the victims rather than the perpetrators of history. "Life," Carlyle argues, "is not given us for the mere sake of Living, but always with an ulterior external Aim." Though we may have limited knowledge of what that aim is and cannot know whether there will be a transcendent reward, we can have some certainty about the conduct that defines the worth of the means by which we strive toward it (*CME*, vol. 3, p. 8). The highest effort expresses innate, non-self-conscious moral energy, whose absence in modern culture Carlyle himself demonstrates in the self-conscious essay that laments the absence.

The eighteenth century and its Victorian extension Carlyle labels

> the reign of Sentimentality . . . when the generous Affections have become well nigh paralytic. The greatness, the profitableness, at any rate the extremely ornamental nature of high feeling, and the luxury of doing good; charity, love, self-forgetfulness, devotedness and all manner of godlike magnanimity,—are everywhere insisted on. [But] were the limbs in right walking order, why so much demonstrating of motion? The barrenest of all mortals is the Sentimentalist. . . . Does he not lie there as a perpetual lesson of despair, and type of bedrid valetudinarian impotence? He is emphatically a Virtue that has become, through every fibre, conscious of itself; it is all sick . . . it can do nothing [except] keep itself alive. (*CME*, vol. 3, pp. 9-10)

Sentimentality manifests the illness of moral reason rather than the health of moral instinct. The inevitable result of attempting to de-mystify is to destroy mystery itself. The antidote is "Nature . . . the bottomless boundless Deep."

Of the Romantic poets, Carlyle, like Dickens, most respected Wordsworth. "The thoughts that do often lie too deep for tears" seemed an expression of the poet's innate moral nature, and Wordsworth's sentimentality had none of the infection of the sensual that Carlyle detected in other Romantic writers. Though cool to Wordsworth the man, whom he thought excessively vain and solipsistic, Carlyle respected Wordsworth's poetry. In contrast, he detested Coleridge on grounds irrelevant to his work. In *The Life of John Sterling* (1851), Carlyle depicted Coleridge's opium addiction and financial dependence as repugnantly immoral, devaluing the artist and human nature. Though as a young man he had studied Byron intently, Carlyle as an adult measured his own maturity by how effective he had been in rejecting Byronic heroism and accepting moral heroism and spiritual hero worship. He thought little of Shelley and less of Keats. Shelley seemed too insubstantial, an airy creature of lyric moonshine and subjective "sensations." Keats seemed erotically obsessed with sensual language, with tactile feeling as self-definition. In most valuing Wordsworth, Carlyle reflected the dominant Victorian preference, and it made no difference that Wordsworth drew much of his tone, rhetoric, and substance about the sentiments from the moral philosophy that Carlyle thought pernicious.

Carlyle was aware that sentimentality in the eighteenth century had divided into two main currents, one associated with sensibility, the other with moral philosophy. By the late part of the century, nurtured by novels such as Sterne's *The Sentimental Journey* and Mackenzie's *The Man of Feeling*, sensibility had become an independent value without any necessary moral content, contributing substantially to the Romantic ethos in poetry and in prose. Actually, Carlyle believed, the sentimental element in Romantic sensibility had nothing to do with Benevolence and moral sentiment. It stressed the heightening of feeling through emotive language in order to authenticate feeling as an affirmation of imagination and being. For Carlyle, only Wordsworth among the Romantics stressed the moral content of feeling, and in terms that had both communal and spiritual dimensions. Wordsworth's moral sensibility had its roots in the poetic tradition—most honored by Carlyle and represented by Homer, Dante, Shakespeare, and Milton—in which the poet had the moral courage of the hero and the spiritual wisdom of the prophet. Sensibility, then, was spiritual potential, the fountainhead of moral energy, the ability to respond to the mysterious truths of "natural supernaturalism," of the divine transcendent force that inheres in ourselves and our world. Wordsworth's sensibility seemed to Carlyle bardic in the great tradition of the poet as seer. The sensibility of the eighteenth-century novelists and the other Romantic poets was self-indulgent, uncontrolled by transcendent forces, a doctrine of feeling for pleasure and self-assertion rather than for religious vision. Carlyle, of course, recognized that Richardson and Fielding had moral aims, and his favorite eighteenth-century novelist, Smollett, had additional virtues. But Carlyle judged the eighteenth century by what he thought both its worst and its dominant temper, and, like Thackeray, he found that in Sterne and Rousseau.

Of the Victorian poets, Carlyle, again like Dickens, most admired Tennyson, especially the early Tennyson. The late Tennyson he thought, among other things, sentimental, particularly *Idylls of the King*, in which "the finely elaborated ex-

ecution" did not disguise "the inward perfection of vacancy
. . . tho the lollipops were so superlative."[10] Though Tennyson did not think of himself or his poetry as sentimental at all,
many of his contemporaries defined his strengths and weak-
nesses in that light. Certainly modern readers have taken one
aspect of sentimentality as a touchstone of Tennyson's art.
Tennyson thought the accusation absurd, and himself deplored Dickens' sentimentality, writing to Elizabeth Barrett
Browning in 1846 that he declined an invitation to accompany
Dickens on holiday in Switzerland because "if I went, I should
be entreating him to dismiss his sentimentality, & so we
should quarrel & part, & never see one another any more."[11]

The early Tennyson seemed to Carlyle in the bardic tradition, his sensibility in the service of mystic experience, of
higher truths. When in the 1840s the two writers became
friends, they argued intensely about personal immortality, in
which Tennyson deeply believed. But they never disagreed
beyond the common ground of a visionary rhetoric that demanded that poetry be both moral exemplar and transcendental experience and that the poet's sensibility be in the service
of cosmic truth. The true poet is of the hero type, soaring
above sensual gratification and rational formulas. The language of poetry has the potential for generating cosmic visions
and the optimism of a regenerative belief system. What Carlyle most admired about Dickens was his cosmic cheerfulness,
though it seemed insufficiently connected to a transcendental
overview. Thackeray seemed to Carlyle unredeemed by either
transcendental vision or cosmic confidence. The balance
sheet, of course, was complicated. Carlyle clearly preferred
Thackeray's social satire to Dickens', judging Thackeray the
more intellectually perceptive of the two. But neither Dickens
nor Thackeray, in Carlyle's judgment, had heroic qualities in

the bardic tradition, as Tennyson did. Neither of them was a transcendent artist. They practiced, in Victorian eyes, the flawed craft of the common day.

Carlyle strongly expressed his disapproval of those aspects of Tennyson's later poetry in which sensibility expresses itself in a language that is both without deep moral feeling and self-consciously self-congratulatory. The Victorians widely acknowledged Tennyson's mastery of sound in poetry, elevating him into a rival of Shakespeare and an equal of Keats. While the comparison with Shakespeare did him no damage, the association with Keats was an unwelcome one. For Carlyle, any significant gap between the appeal of language as sound and the appeal of poetry as moral wisdom created sentimentality in the worst sense, feeling in excess of what the dramatic situation supports and sensuality without appropriate moral content. Carlyle admired Tennyson's *Poems* of 1842, particularly "Ulysses," because he felt the consonance between the poetic language and the moral content. To Tennyson's mid-Victorian audience, his great gifts seemed in the service of the highest ideals, duty, heroic striving, and moral responsibility. They thought "Ulysses," whatever ambivalence modern critics may read into it, a brilliant presentation of the dialectic between stasis and movement, a celebration of patriarchal authority, generational continuity, and responsible work. Tennyson celebrated the Victorian worker in the vineyard of the Lord, and the poet as worker defined his sensibility as both mystic and moral.

That Tennyson's popularity actually increased after the publication of his domestic idylls and during the publication of *Idylls of the King* seemed to Carlyle unfortunate evidence that his contemporaries had lost whatever sharpness of judgment, standards of poetry, and heroic values they had had.

Tennyson's later poems appealed to sentimentality rather than sensibility, substituting the moral sentiments for transcendent moral vision. Tennyson became, in Carlyle's view, more like Dickens and Thackeray than like Homer, Dante, Shakespeare, and Milton. Attempting to create epic poetry based on Arthurian materials, he created domestic poetry. Attempting to create narrative poetry, he created sentimental tales whose definitions of human nature derived from simplistic theories of natural goodness. In Carlyle's judgment, the moral base for action had become separated from the visionary perception of cosmic mystery.

~———❧ 4 ☙———❧

Sincerity, the ultimate virtue that precedes all others, is, for Carlyle, the enemy of sentimentality. The discourse of eighteenth-century life and literature was, in Carlyle's judgment, insincere. At best it was contaminated by the imperception of an age of disbelief. In Carlyle's terms, one cannot be a rationalist and also be sincere, unless one defines sincerity in the limited sense of "honesty." Samuel Johnson was honest, deeply so. But sincerity necessitates spiritual depth, and in this regard Johnson's honesty could not possibly take him deep enough. Sincerity is like an electric current; its power source is spiritual vision and cosmic mystery. All good literature, Carlyle proposes, is "honest." But great literature is sincere as well.

On the basis of his doctrine of sincerity, Carlyle created a theory of literature that gives primacy to the consonance between the power of language and moral action. It is based on a revitalization of the traditional claim that in the beginning was the word; the word was not separated or disassociated from action. In fact, language was action, articulation was identical to and subject to the same principles as deed. Consequently, the words of the Bard, instinctively sincere, part of the mystic energy of the world, were active forces, doing work in the world. Sincerity, of course, *means* moral vision *and* moral action inseparably together. For Carlyle, sentimentality is insincerity, moral feeling without moral action, either simply insufficient—the result of not trying hard enough—or dishonest, or, at worst, perversely evil and unnatural. "Insincere Speech, truly, is the prime material of insincere Action. Action hangs, as it were, dissolved in Speech, in Thought, whereof Speech is the Shadow, and precipitates itself therefrom. The Kind of Speech in a man betokens the kind of Action you will get from him" (*PP*, Part II, p. 151).

Carlyle believed that literature is a self-reflexive language expression that must be simultaneously word and act, speech and action. For literature's mission is to bring language and belief into consonance, to establish their true, original unity; to rid the world of falsehood. Sincerity, then, inheres in the relationship between the words and the belief system that the words enact and that demands enactment. But how can one distinguish sincerity from insincerity? How can one identify the degree of consistency between the words and the intent to act on their import that will make the words acts, that will enable one to distinguish between sincerity as an identifiable virtue and degrees of sincerity that are less than absolute? With characteristic radicalism, Carlyle demands the absolute as the minimum level. All utterance that is not absolutely sincere fails in sincerity, though not all insincere speech is dishonest since not all belief systems are equal. To the extent that an author attempts to unify language and a false belief system, he may at least be "honest," the unwitting victim of his society's delusions. Such an artist can never be fully sincere since he has been given flawed, false materials to work with. Carlyle, though, chafes at the conclusion that cultural givens absolutely control our potential for sincerity, that there can be no prophets in an age of reason and during the "reign of sentimentality." Without fully relieving Johnson of his cultural disability, Carlyle, in "The Hero as Man of Letters," allows that this great victim, "whose ideas are fast becoming obsolete," had the greatest amount of sincerity that his age could permit. "It was in virtue of his *sincerity*, of his speaking still in some sort from the heart of Nature, though in the current artificial dialect, that Johnson was a Prophet" (*HHW*, chap. 5, p. 180).

In Carlyle's view, the writer always practices a discipline of action more problematic in regard to its sincerity than that of the priest and the king, partly because the writer cannot avoid self-consciousness. The novelist in particular confronts special difficulties. The Hero as Priest has a sanctioned liturgy and text by which the consonance between his speech and belief can readily be tested. The Hero as King, who must focus on the realities of the physical world, synthesizes word and act in the dramatic spotlight of public assessment. The modern writer, however, whether novelist or poet, constantly runs the danger, in a secular world of fragmented belief systems, of being honest rather than sincere and of not having the means to know the difference. Consequently, Carlyle promotes, in the modern crisis, total reliance on instinct rather than craft or *kunst*, on the assumption that the Hero has inherent within him, as Samuel Johnson had, some portion of divinity that not even a secular, mechanistic culture can fully repress. But the novelist, who deals with the tactile details of daily life, runs

the special risk of depicting the material world as self-suffi-
cient or of interpreting its details as manifestations of a false
ideology or of taking refuge in the solipsism of feeling or sentimentality in which feeling is separated from moral structure
and control. Since the novelist has a special mandate to mediate between concrete particulars and moral idealizations, it
is more difficult for the novelist in the nineteenth century than
for the poet or the writer of nonfictional prose to be sincere
in the way that Carlyle believes sincerity is the essence of
greatness.

〜━━◄ဇ 5 ٯ◄━━━

Carlyle's tolerance for sentimentality was greater in fact than
his principles would seem to permit. Two elements within his
writing are noticeably sentimental, his emphasis on his own
feelings as self-evidently moral and his creation of moral ideals in his concept of the heroic. The Victorians in general did
not consciously label their commitment to heroic models as an
idealization or an affirmation of the innate moral nature of human nature. But Carlyle would not have been puzzled at an
extrapolation from a belief in the heroic as innately good that
concludes that there is a primal, innate goodness within human nature that makes it capable of responding to heroic
models. Actually, though goodness is a word he uses frequently, Carlyle is not comfortable with the concept, primarily because it promotes a rhetoric, a set of problems, and a
definition of human nature that do not suit his temperament
or his vision. The idealized characters of the literature of
moral philosophy are good in the ethical sense that Carlyle rejects. It is not at all sentimental, he believes, to create ideali-

zations whose heroic dimensions express the spiritual forces of nature and the cosmos. But it is pejoratively sentimental to create characters whose totality can be encompassed within the boundaries of ethics. Carlyle deals with an upper case, Dickens and Thackeray with a lower case, Universe. For Carlyle, it is not our goodness that we have lost contact with but our divinity.

Carlyle, then, had as much trouble with the novel as a literary form as he had with any specific work of that genre, a work such as *Vanity Fair*, for example, which announced itself as "A Novel Without A Hero." A perceptive literary critic, he was sufficiently aware of genre assumptions and demands to realize that the novel could not function effectively without being solidly anchored in the social world. But, though he admired the brilliant satiric anatomy of society in *Vanity Fair*, he attached more value to the moral allegory and spiritual vision of *Pilgrim's Progress*, the work from which the title of the novel derived, than to Thackeray's depiction of the faulty machinery of society. What Carlyle did not hear in the novel as a genre was the cosmic voice, the voice of ultimate sincerity, beyond goodness because it was beyond ethics, the divine voice that speaks in man. Such a voice expresses unconscious primal nature, the strongest innate element of human nature, the ultimate model for all life which in its creative mysteries contains both life and death. To deny that voice is to be insincere, a sham, a falsity. Not to hear it at all is to have lost the faculty of hearing or to have had one's hearing diminished by a false culture's noise and static. The primal voice can hardly be heard in the modern novel, Carlyle maintains, because the form itself limits the hearing, decreasing the full range of decibels, and those who have been attracted to the form have become successful practitioners precisely because of the consonance between their personal disabilities and the genre's limitations. Only if we listen intently, Carlyle suggests, will we be able to perceive just slightly the distant ranges of the cosmic voice in *certain* novels, so powerfully and irrepressibly primal is that voice to the language of genius.

Carlyle believed, as did Dickens and Thackeray, that the greatest danger to the human community was the increasing devaluation of human nature, either in mechanical, secular, or biological forms. The result was a loss of confidence in the innate goodness or divinity—or both—of human nature. Of course, it made considerable difference to many sectarian Victorians, including Carlyle, whether the assertion of the human capacity to act *well* takes its force from moral philosophy or from spiritual vision, whether it is expressed within the boundaries of realistic fiction or within the limitlessness of a transcendent cosmos.

Still, there was general agreement that the opponents of moral sentiment and religious vision, in the process of creating the social and physical sciences, defined mankind as the product of either historical environment or random physical forces; and that repressive social conditions were narrowing moral responsiveness, grinding it in the secular mills and casting it aside contemptuously as the illusion of the Sabbath rather than the reality of the weekday. The Victorian sentimentalists, and particularly Dickens and Thackeray, affirmed the fragile hope that human beings, in their instinctive natures, innately know right from wrong, and that at the level of innate response they take pleasure in the triumph of goodness and the defeat of evil in literature and in life. These Victorian sentimentalists trusted that the source of "sacred tears" was the moral spring of human nature. It would water flowers no matter how arid the soil.

Notes

All citations from Dickens' novels are from the *Oxford Illustrated Dickens* (London: 1948–64) except those from the novels *Oliver Twist, Dombey and Son, Little Dorrit*, and *David Copperfield*, which appear in *The Clarendon Dickens* (Oxford: 1966, 1974, 1979, 1981), and those from the novels *Hard Times* and *Bleak House*, which appear in the Norton Critical Edition series (New York: 1966, 1977). Quotations from Thackeray are from *The Oxford Thackeray With Illustrations*, edited by George Saintsbury (London: 1908), with the exception of those from *Vanity Fair*, which are from the Riverside edition (Boston: 1963), edited by Geoffrey and Kathleen Tillotson. Since the volumes in *The Oxford Thackeray* are not numbered, I have indicated for essays and other short pieces the title of the volume in which each appears. The Carlyle quotations are from *The Centenary Edition of Carlyle's Works* (London: 1896–99).

Notes to Chapter One

1. *Tom Jones*, ed. Martin C. Battestin and Fredson Bowers (Middletown, Conn.: 1975), 7:1. All references to *Tom Jones* and *Joseph Andrews* are to *The Wesleyan Edition of the Works of Henry Fielding*, edited by Battestin and Bowers.

2. Thomas Hobbes, *Leviathan* (1651; Indianapolis: 1958), Part II, chap. 17, p. 139.

3. *Joseph Andrews*, ed. Martin C. Battestin and Fredson Bowers (Middletown, Conn.: 1967), p. 9.

4. The subject is indeed more complicated than the *OED* entry reflects, mainly because of the complex cultural history that adheres

to words and phrases such as sentiment, sentimental, sentimentality, the sentimental novel, sensibility, and the man of sensibility or feeling. In both its sparsity and unhelpfulness, the literature on the subject reflects its elusiveness, especially the difficulty of consistent definitions. Erick Erametsa's *A Study of the Word "Sentimental"* (Helsinki: 1951) does not resolve the difficulties. Barbara Hardy, in *Forms of Feeling in Victorian Fiction* (Athens, Ohio: 1985), deals with Dickens' sentimentality in non-Victorian terms. Among those general works on the subject that I have found helpful are Northrop Frye, "Toward Defining an Age of Sensibility," in *Eighteenth Century English Literature, Modern Essays in Criticism* (Oxford: 1959), pp. 311-18; Louis I. Bredvold, *The Natural History of Sensibility* (Detroit: 1962); R. F. Brissenden, *Virtue in Distress: Studies in the Novel of Sentiment from Richardson to Sade* (New York: 1974); Robert Bledsoe, *"Pendennis* and the Power of Sentimentality: A Study of Motherly Love," *PMLA* 91 (1976), 846-55; Richard O. Allen, "If You Have Tears: Sentimentalism as Soft Romanticism," *Genre* 8 (1977), 119-45; G. A. Starr, " 'Only A Boy': Notes on Sentimental Novels," *Genre* 8 (1977), 501-27; William J. Palmer, "Dickens and the Eighteenth Century," *Dickens Studies Annual*, ed. R. B. Partlow, 6 (1977), 15-39; and John Irving, "In Defense of Sentimentality," *New York Times Book Review*, 25 November 1980, p. 3.

5. David Hume, *Essays and Treatises on Several Subjects* (London: 1825), 2:331, 198. This edition, quite popular in the Victorian period, is the one that Dickens owned.

6. Adam Smith, *The Theory of Moral Sentiments* (Edinburgh: 1759), ed. E. G. West (Indianapolis: 1969), 3:204-5, 228-29, 234-35. In *David Copperfield*, Micawber claims that his exertions to expose Heep's crimes were "stimulated by the silent monitor within, and by a no less touching and appealing monitor without" (chap. 52).

7. William Makepeace Thackeray, *The English Humourists of the Eighteenth Century*, chap. 4, p. 620.

8. Alexander Pope, *Essay on Man* (1733–34); in *The Poems of Alex-*

ander Pope, ed. Maynard Mack (New Haven: 1950), vol. 2, Epistle I, p. 292; Epistle II, pp. 175, 217-18, 231-32.

9. Pope, *Essay on Man*, Epistle II, p. 183.

10. Daniel Defoe, *A Journal of the Plague Year* (1722), in *Oxford English Novels*, ed. Louis Landa (Oxford: 1968), p. 165.

11. Daniel Defoe, *Moll Flanders* (1722), in *Oxford English Novels*, ed. G. A. Starr (Oxford: 1971), p. 278. *The Political History of the Devil* (1726), in *The Novels and Miscellaneous Works of Defoe* (London: 1840), 10:368 and *passim*.

12. Anthony Earl of Shaftesbury, *Characteristics of Men, Manners, Opinions, Times, etc.* (1711), ed. John M. Robertson (London: 1963), 1:309, 317.

13. Francis Hutcheson, *An Essay Concerning the Principles and Conduct of the Passions and Affections* (1725, 1728, 1742), reprint of 1742 ed., ed. Paul McReynolds (Gainesville: 1969), pp. 236, 204-5.

14. David Hume, *An Inquiry Concerning the Principles of Morals* (1751), ed. Charles W. Hendel (Indianapolis: 1957), p. 105.

15. *Joseph Andrews*, p. 188.

16. *Joseph Andrews*, p. 324.

17. Lady Bradshaigh to Samuel Richardson, 9 January 1750. Quoted in William Lynn Phelps, "Richardson's Influence," in Samuel Richardson, *The History of Clarissa Harlow* (London: 1901), 1:x.

18. Dickens owned a five-volume edition of *Goldsmith's Works* (1792). The edition of record is *Collected Works of Oliver Goldsmith*, ed. Arthur Friedman (Oxford: 1966). Richard H. Hopkins, in *The True Genius of Oliver Goldsmith* (Baltimore: 1969), argues that the *Vicar* is a satire whose prime target is Primrose.

19. John Forster, *The Life and Times of Oliver Goldsmith* (London: 1848; 2d ed. 1854), vol. 2, bk. 13, pp. 3, 15.

20. Boswell, quoted from *Life of Johnson*, bk. 3, pp. 95-96, in Forster, *Life of Goldsmith*, vol. 2, bk. 6, p. 308.

21. Edwin Eigner, in *The Metaphysical Novel in England and America: Dickens, Bulwer, Hawthorne, Melville* (Berkeley: 1978), presents the most effective analysis I have read of the anti-realistic novel in the nineteenth century.

Notes to Chapter Two

Notes to Chapter Two

1. Letter from Dickens to Angela Coutts, 29 March 1849, in *The Pilgrim Edition of the Letters of Charles Dickens*, ed. Graham Storey and K. J. Fielding (Oxford: 1981), 5:517.

2. *Joseph Andrews*, p. 10.

3. *Pilgrim* (1965), ed. Madeline House and Graham Storey, 1:639.

4. *Pilgrim* (1974), ed. Madeline House, Graham Storey, and Kathleen Tillotson, 3:57, n. 7.

5. Letter from Dickens to John Forster, 2 March 1842, in *Pilgrim*, 3:211.

6. Richard Henry Horne, *The New Spirit of the Age* (London: 1844, 1907), pp. 46-47.

7. Henry Hallam, quoted in R. C. Churchill, *A Bibliography of Dickensian Criticism, 1836–1976* (New York: 1975), pp. 183-84.

8. R. H. Hutton, quoted in Churchill, *Dickensian Criticism*, p. 184.

9. William Dodd, *Reflections on Death* (London: 1763), pp. 5-6.

10. Dodd, *Reflections on Death*, p. 62.

11. Boswell, quoted from *Life of Johnson*, bk. 3, pp. 95-99, in Forster, *Life of Goldsmith*, 1:308.

12. Arthur Hugh Clough, "Recent English Poetry," *The North American Review* 77 (1853), 1-30. Quoted in Park Honan, *Matthew Arnold, A Life* (New York: 1981), p. 282.

13. See Humphry House, *The Dickens World* (Oxford: 1941), pp. 36-54, and William Palmer, "Dickens and the Eighteenth Century," in *Dickens Studies Annual*, ed. R. B. Partlow, 6 (1977), 15-39.

14. Smith, *Theory of Moral Sentiments*, p. 208.

15. Smith, *Theory of Moral Sentiments*, p. 212.

16. Smith, *Theory of Moral Sentiments*, p. 212.

17. Hume, *Essays and Treatises*, pp. 327-28.

18. Letter from Dickens to Wilkie Collins, 13 July 1856, in *The*

Nonesuch Edition of the Letters of Charles Dickens, ed. Walter Dexter (London: 1938), 2:792.

19. Matthew Arnold, "To An Independent Preacher."

Notes to Chapter Three

1. Jane Ellen Frith Panton, *Leaves From A Life* (London: 1908), pp. 150-51.

2. William Makepeace Thackeray, "Charity and Humour," added to the New York edition of *The English Humourists of the Eighteenth Century* (New York: 1853). It appears in *Christmas Books, Rebecca and Rowena, and Late Minor Papers, 1849–1861*, pp. 626, 628.

3. Thackeray, "Charity and Humour," p. 617.

4. *The Letters and Private Papers of William Makepeace Thackeray*, comp and ed. Gordon N. Ray (Cambridge, Mass: 1945), 2:772-73.

5. See John Stonehouse, *Catalogue of the Libraries of Charles Dickens and William Thackeray* (London: 1935).

6. *Thackeray's Contributions to the Morning Chronicle*, ed. Gordon N. Ray (Urbana, Ill.: 1955), p. 114.

7. *Letters and Private Papers*, 1:56, 166; 2:234.

8. Smith, *Theory of Moral Sentiments*, pp. 204-5.

9. William Makepeace Thackeray, "Fielding's Works," *The Times*, 2 September 1840. It appears in *Catherine, A Shabby Genteel Story, The Second Funeral of Napoleon and Miscellanies, 1840-1841*, p. 383.

10. See Gordon N. Ray, *Thackeray, The Age of Wisdom 1847–1863* (New York: 1958), pp. 148-56.

11. Thackeray, "Fielding's Works," p. 387. See E.D.H. Johnson, "*Vanity Fair* and *Amelia*: Thackeray in the Perspective of the Eighteenth Century," *Modern Philology* 59 (1961), 100-113.

12. Thackeray, "Fielding's Works," p. 386.

13. Thackeray, "Charity and Humour," p. 625.
14. Thackeray, "Charity and Humour," p. 627.

Notes to Chapter Four

1. I have chosen these passages because, among other reasons, they are those used by Russell A. Fraser in "Sentimentality in Thackeray's *The Newcomes*," *Nineteenth-Century Fiction* 4 (December 1949), 187-96, as examples of Thackeray's sentimentality. Fraser assumes that his readers know what sentimentality is, and that they think it bad in various ways.

2. See Ray, *Thackeray, The Age of Wisdom*, p. 424.

3. Partly because of his birth, his education, and his interest in the "moral gentleman," Thackeray is less engaged than Dickens and Carlyle with the problems of work, either practical or theoretical. Dobbin, of course, works; the army is a profession. Pendennis struggles with Grub Street. Thackeray himself faced admirably the challenge of working to support himself and his family after the loss of his inheritance. But the general attitude toward work expressed in Thackeray's fiction is that it does not really contribute to moral definition, that neither personal nor social salvation depends upon it. Unlike Dickens and Carlyle, Thackeray is more interested in tone than in effort, and he seems at most mildly concerned with Tennyson's Carlylean notion of "use and name and fame," an allusion to the artist and art as having an *active* social dimension.

4. George Brinsely, *Essays*, ed. William George Clark (London: 1882), p. 256.

Notes to Chapter Five

1. *New Letters of Thomas Carlyle*, ed. Alexander Carlyle (London: 1904), 2:122.

2. See "Phallus-Worship" (1848), MS., Hilles Collection, Beinecke Library, Yale University, and Fred Kaplan, " 'Phallus-Worship' (1848): A Response to the Revolution of 1848," *Carlyle Newsletter* 2 (1980), 19-23.

3. William Blake, "Mock On Mock On Voltaire Rousseau."

4. *The Collected Letters of Thomas and Jane Welsh Carlyle*, Duke-Edinburgh ed., ed. Charles R. Sanders and K. J. Fielding (Durham, N.C.: 1970), 7:54-55.

5. See Charles R. Sanders, "The Byron Closed in *Sartor Resartus*," *Studies in Romanticism* 3 (1964), 77-108.

6. Ray, *Thackeray, The Age of Wisdom*, p. 191.

7. See Kaplan, "Phallus-Worship," p. 22.

8. See Fred Kaplan, "Carlyle's Marginalia and George Henry Lewes' Fiction," *Carlyle Newsletter* 5 (1984), 21-27.

9. *New Letters and Memorials of Jane Welsh Carlyle*, ed. Alexander Carlyle (London: 1903), 2:47.

10. *The Correspondence of Emerson and Carlyle*, ed. Joseph Slater (New York: 1946), pp. 552-53.

11. *The Letters of Robert Browning and Elizabeth Barrett Browning, 1845–1846*, ed. Elvan Kintner (Cambridge, Mass: 1969), 2:667.

Index

Index

Library of Congress Cataloging-in-Publication Data

Kaplan, Fred, 1937-
Sacred tears.

Includes index.
1. English literature—19th century—History and criticism.   2.
Sentimentalism in literature.   3. Crying in literature.   4. Ethics in
literature.   5. Dickens, Charles, 1812–1870—Criticism and
interpretation.   6. Thackeray, William Makepeace, 1811–1863—
Criticism and interpretation.   7. Carlyle, Thomas, 1795–1881—
Criticism and interpretation.   I. Title.
PR468.S46K36   1987   820'.9'353   86–22548

ISBN 0–691–06700–7 (alk. paper)